Postca of Old Hull

by

Christopher Ketchell

Hutton Press
1997

Published by

The Hutton Press Ltd.,
130 Canada Drive, Cherry Burton,
Beverley, East Yorkshire HU17 7SB

Printed by
Image Colourprint Ltd.,
Grange Park Lane,
Willerby, Hull
HU10 6EB

ISBN 1 872167 93 4

Contents

FOREWORD

I was honoured and delighted to be asked to contribute a foreword to this book, but even more delighted to see this volume in print.

Working for the past 25 years in local newspapers in Hull I have been constantly in the debt of people like Chris Ketchell for their encyclopedic knowledge of the city; its history and people. Chris's passion for Hull burns brighter than most; in the early days I remember his efforts, via the Help! Conservation Action Group, to try to persuade developers and planners to save more of the wonderful buildings in the Old Town.

It was around that time, as the columnist "John Humber" of the Hull Daily Mail, I remember Chris introducing me to a wonderful book about old shopfronts and from that grew a series about city shops in the paper based on his extensive photographic collection. I was to return to that collection time and time again over the ensuing years whenever I needed help with the many nostalgia series to have appeared in papers like the Hull Star, Target and Advertiser and the Mail's own special supplements.

And it was just last year that the Mail produced two Flashback specials called "Postcards From Hull & the East Riding", based almost totally on his collection. Needless to say they were extremely well received and sold well; as I am sure this book will.

Postcards, as all collectors will testify, are a unique reference to how a particular location looked in the early days of this century and Hull has been particularly well served in that respect. In this volume you will see City Centre and Old Town locations, house and shop portraits from points north, west, and east, statues and churches, the docks, sporting and war-time heroes and, most important of all, Hull's own people.

This book is a testament to Chris's love and knowledge of Hull and its history; by his efforts we all have easy access to an archive to help us understand our heritage and where we are today. Future generations will have even more reason to value his efforts.

Roy Woodcock

INTRODUCTION

How many postcards of Hull are there? How many grains of sand are there on the beach?! We will never know!

Many tens, if not hundreds of thousands of postcards of Hull must have been published during the height of the Edwardian postcard craze, say between say 1903 and the outbreak of the First World War. Nationally, 93 million postcards were sent through the postal system in 1905, which seems to be the most common date found on most old picture postcards.

The first old postcards I was ever aware of were those in the collection of my Granny Ketchell, and although the album which I`m sure they must have been in, has not survived, I do have a few of the cards which were sent between members of the family.

The first postcards I became aware of as 'collectors` items' were some I saw in an antiques shop at Stepney on Beverley Road in Hull whilst buying furniture for my first flat when I moved to live in Hull in 1968. The source was presumably a 'house clearance' and I began buying a few of these cards, not initially concentrating on Hull but collecting for quite a wide area, including up the coast as far as Scarborough and Whitby and out into East Yorkshire. My area of interest gradually expanded until I was collecting cards for quite a large area centred on Hull but spreading out up the coast into North Yorkshire and down into Lincolnshire and inland to cover all of East Yorkshire and some parts of West Yorkshire. I built up collections for Scarborough, Whitby, Bridlington, Driffield where I lived before moving to Hull, and of course Hull.

My interests in local history and local affairs developed in the early 1970s and I joined a Workers Educational Association local history class with Mr. William Foot Walker as the tutor, and began to discuss postcards with him. Occasionally I would be invited to his house in Westbourne Avenue to look at his old books, pictures and postcards. I was lucky enough to inherit some of his collection of postcards following his death in 1995. I recall he was horrified at the price I had to pay then for the old postcards, perhaps a shilling or one and sixpence (5p or 7$1/_2$p for those of you who cannot relate to 'real money'!) As far as he was concerned, postcards cost 2d or 3d (1p)!

Over the years I have successively restricted my area of interest as far as collecting postcards is concerned and I really no longer consider myself as a collector. I do not actively seek the postcards out, but often as part of my work as supervisor of the Local History Unit at the Park Street Centre of Hull College, the postcards seek me out! I am always pleased to be shown a collection, however large or small; even the smallest collection of local cards will include some I have never seen before. I do now try to concentrate on Hull cards, but even so, now and then there are 'gems' for other areas, perhaps King`s Mill at Driffield or a never-before-seen methodist chapel in an East Riding village, which I cannot resist. For a brief period I attempted to collect postcards of all the pleasure piers in the country, an enterprise doomed to failure, as there seemed to be some so rare one would never find them. Initially I wrote to dealers who advertised in magazines like Exchange and Mart who would send you their lists of cards for sale and sometimes would even send them on approval. Gradually the trade developed and specialist dealers, shops and magazines and books began to appear. However I soon discovered that although as a collector I liked the 'object' or artefact, the old postcard itself; it was the historical information contained within the image on the card which was of most value to me as a local historian. I copied old picture postcards on to transparencies and used them to illustrate my slide shows on topics as diverse as Pearson Park, the history of Anlaby Road, Hull`s Old Town, Prince`s Avenue, Cinemas and Theatres, Shops, Hull`s Docks - all these subjects illustrated on old picture postcards. Prices gradually, or on occasion rapidly, increased and I could no longer afford to buy the 'best' cards, those rare real photographic cards which one had never-seen-before. When deciding not to buy one of these rare real photographic cards one had to realise that it would probably never be seen again, as it was unique. How many of these individual cards were published at the time? Six, a dozen, ten, fifty? We do not know. As far as I am aware no postcard publisher or photographer`s records have survived locally to provide any information about such questions.

However there is no question that given the time one can find a myriad of local subjects illustrated on picture postcards, both those produced by the national postcard publishing firms like Valentines, and the many local photographers and postcard publishers. There are many dozens if not hundreds of postcards of such scenes as Prince`s Dock, Queen Victoria Square and the City Hall, the Town Hall, the Pier, King Edward Street, the Market Place, Holy Trinity Church and the Parks. I dare not buy a postcard of one of these subjects now as I`ve probably already acquired it many years ago (maybe for the same number of pence as one would now have to pay pounds!). All these subjects are covered in this book. However to the collector, and the local historian it is the rarer cards of the 'back streets', shopfronts, railway stations, industries and of course the 'lost pubs' which are the eagerly sort-after gems. Most of these categories are included along with other popular subjects for postcard publishers such as 'disasters', the E13 submarine and 'Russian Outrage' cards being local examples.

I find myself increasingly intrigued with the messages on the back (if you are a postcard collector, but 'front' if you are a philatelist!) of the postcards. It`s like listening-in to someone`s private conversation or telephone call, and I have included a number of these snippets of life from the past.

Many friends and colleagues have helped with the compilation of this collection of postcards and I am grateful to them all for their valued assistance. Others have loaned postcards from their own collections, although the majority are from my own collection, and their help is recorded in the acknowledgements. I have included a comprehensive bibliography and I recommend you to explore these sources of information about postcards and local history. If you like the views included in Postcards of Old Hull, please let me know by sending me a postcard!

Christopher Ketchell
Kingston upon Hull
October 1997

Dedication

For my friends and teachers; Roy Dresser; the late John Meadley; David Neave; Leslie Powell; the late Eric Sigsworth; Ted Tuxworth; the late William Foot Walker

1. THE OLD TOWN

MARKET PLACE, HULL

Market Place, Hull
Brumby & Clarke, Ltd., Art Printers, Hull and London
p/u 1906
This coloured locally produced printed p/c shows the east side of the Market Place with Varley`s Cross Keys Hotel prominent in the centre. The statue of King William III, "King Billy", and his famous underground toilets can be seen in the middle of a busy street scene surrounded by delivery vans and carts, an open-topped electric tram, and a hansom cab. St. Mary`s Church, Lowgate can be seen in the distance. All the buildings on the right have since been replaced by the modern King William House and multi-storey car-park. The present bleak Market Place shows no resemblance to this busy attractive scene.

MARKET PLACE, HULL.

Market Place, Hull
b/w no publisher p/u 1904
The message on this p/c is written in shorthand, presumably in an attempt to keep the message from the postman (or woman)! This view of the west side of the Market Place shows the shops between the King Billy public house just off the picture to the left and the corner of South Church Side. Beyond the east front of Holy Trinity Church can be seen the now missing property at the corner of North Church Side, next to the Old Corn Exchange public house.

Market Place from S., Hull

Market Place from South, Hull
Valentine`s Series not p/u sepia with border

Market Place from North, Hull
Valentine`s Series not p/u sepia with border
The Medieval Marketgate.

Market Place from North, Hull

Market Place, Hull
Valentine`s 65836
Another busy scene is shown on this view of the Market Place, the medieval Market Gate, looking south into Queen Street; on the right is the corner of Mytongate and centre left can be seen the Market Hall or Shambles. Construction of the South Orbital Road, now Castle Street, Garrison Road and Myton Bridge destroyed the enclosed nature of the south end of the Market Place leaving the golden statue of King William III ("King Billy") stranded in the midst of busy traffic. Note the somewhat wet and muddy state of the road, and think of the mess which would have been left behind by all those horse-drawn carts!

Whitefriargate, Hull
p/u 1904 sent from the Royal Station Hotel with the message *"Have you seen this place before! Am working here valuing the docks and North Eastern Railway..."*

In A High Street Court
PB.146

A typical view of the appearance of much of the housing in the Old Town, built from the late 18th Century and early 19th Century in small courts off the main street, often on medieval alignments. Access to these courts was usually through a tunnel-entrance under the building facing the street. Very little property of this sort survives in the Old Town now, Scott's Square between Blanket Row and Humber Street was demolished only recently. This view may be of Stewart's Yard. The bow-windowed house may have been a shop, but the presence of the large lamp could perhaps imply the presence of a 'lost pub'. [P]

At Hull`s Old Watergate, Humber Street

A posed photograph of the entrance to Little Lane from Humber Street which gave access to Blackfriargate and formed part of the route from the landing place, from the Humber, at the South End, to the centre of the Old Town. It was reputed to be 'the Watergate' entrance through the medieval town walls, and often considered to be part of the town's brick walls, although this does not seem likely as the walls probably ran along the south side of Humber Street. The brick arch, which certainly incorporated very old bricks, survived the demolition of the Blitz-damaged property of which it latterly formed part, and probably pre-dated, but was demolished to extend a lorry park in the late 1960s, when Little Lane itself was also closed. To the left, west, of the "Old Watergate" was another of the Old Town`s 'Lost Pubs', The Labour in Vain, later Tiger No.6. [P]

2. THE DOCKS

Queen`s Dock, Hull

Dania Glossy Real Photograph, The Doncaster Rotophoto Co., Ltd.

not p/u

This view is looking west along the length of Queen`s Dock from the lock-pit entrance from the River Hull towards the Dock Offices at the western end.

The Dock with $9^3/_4$ acres of water space was opened at a cost of £83,335 in 1778. Prior to 1774 the wharf and quays used for shipping were on the River Hull adjacent to the warehouses which the wealthy merchants built behind their houses in High Street. Legal quays were established at other ports in the reigns of Elizabeth I and Charles II and in 1746 the Customs Commissioners reported that if their work was to be carried out properly, it was necessary for legal quays to be established at Hull. Nothing was done until the commissioners of Customs threatened in 1772 to establish a dock and quays elsewhere on the Humber. Subsequently the Dock Company at Kingston upon Hull was formed in 1773, and the new company obtained their first Act of Parliament to make a dock or basin to extend from the River Hull to Beverley Gate. They received from the Crown for dock purposes "the gates, walls, buildings, inner and outer ditches, ramparts and bastions, bridges and bridgeways" extending from North Gate to the Hessle Gate. Parliament also granted £15,000 towards defraying the expenses of the undertaking. The first stone of The Dock was laid on 19 October 1775 by Joseph Outram the then mayor, and the dock was opened on 22 September 1778.

Queen`s Dock, Hull

A busy scene with shipping in Queen`s Dock. Is the date the eary 1930s? The trawlers, laid up in the background, include the 'Ganton' built by Cochrane & Son, Selby, with engines by C.D. Holmes & Co. Ltd., Hull, owned by S. Collinson. The trawler, Register number 110 appears in the Lloyds Registers from 1914 to 1930/31.

Originally known simply as The Dock, when a second dock, Humber Dock was opened in 1809 the name changed to Old Dock until in 1854 the dock`s name was changed to Queen`s Dock as a compliment to Queen Victoria who visited Hull that year.

The Humber Dock, Hull

The Humber Dock, Hull

The second of Hull's docks to be constructed, Humber Dock, the first stone being laid on 13 April 1807 and the dock was opened on 30 June 1809, at a cost of £233,086 and provided $7^1/_4$ acres of water space. Humber Dock closed in 1968 and it is now part of the Marina, opened in 1983.

Dock Offices & Wilberforce Monument, Hull

This view of Prince's Dock looking north from the Mytongate lock-pit towards Monument Bridge.

The postcard has an undivided back which suggests a date of pre-1902.

Work on the construction of the third of Hull's docks Junction Dock; it joined together Old Dock and Humber Dock; commenced with the first stone of the south lock being laid on 10 December 1827 and the dock opened on 1 June 1829. The name was changed to Prince's Dock in 1854 after the Royal visit.

Dock Offices & Wilberforce Monument. Hull.

Kingston upon Hull Princes Dock

Photo by J.F. Lawrence Is the date perhaps c1950s?

A very similar view of Prince's Dock, but many years later. This view shows the changes which have taken place. St. John's church has been replaced by the Ferens Art Gallery, Wilberforce Monument has neen removed to its present site at the east end of Queen's Gardens, the Hull Brewery chimney has appeared on the skyline, and Monument Buildings of 1908 and Bridge Chambers of 1914 have been built, as has the Burton's Building of 1935. Prince's Dock closed in 1968, and Prince's Quay shopping centre was built, partly covering the dock, between 1987-`90, opening on 15 March 1991.

Victoria Dock, Hull

W&S

Victoria Dock the first dock to be built east of the River Hull was opened in 1850 and closed in 1970. The dock, which had become the centre of the timber importing industry, was then filled in and the area has recently been developed with housing as the Victoria Dock 'village'.

VICTORIA DOCK. HULL (W&S)

Dock Offices & Wilberforce Monument. Hull.

Albert Dock, Hull
Valentines Series coloured p/c
not p/u
Albert Dock opened on 22 July 1869, by HRH Prince Albert, was built at a cost of £1,009,746 and with an area of water of $24^1/_2$ acres was then the largest of Hull's docks. It was initially to be known as West Dock, hence West Dock Avenue and West Dock Street leading to the dock which is still in use.

Albert Dock
Valentines Series 75453 not p/u
This view looking west shows the clock tower of the Riverside Quay, of 1907, on the left and large dockside warehouses on the right, north side, which have since been demolished.

Albert Dock, Hull

Alexandra Dock, Hull

A Valentines Series coloured postcard

Alexandra Dock of 46 acres was built by the Hull, Barnsley and West Riding Junction Railway and Dock Company, in 1885 at a cost of £1,355,392. The dock was described by Brown`s Illustrated Guide in 1891 as being "2,300 feet in length, 1,000 feet wide and contains a water space of $46^1/2$ acres. This is an immense water space compared with any of the older docks, and the advantage of its great length and width are increased by the depth of water, which is 34 feet 6 inches. The entrance to the dock is bell-mouthed, and the lock, which is a really splendid structure, is 550 feet in length, with a width of 85 feet. All steamers and sailing vessels of ordinary tonnage can be locked into the dock at any state of the tide, an advantage unknown here until the formation of this dock. For situation, extent and facilities for the accomodation of ships of the greatest tonnage this dock stands almost unrivalled, being second only to Tilbury Dock on the Thames. The substantial character of every prominent feature of the undertaking is apparent to every one, whilst all that modern engineering skill and experience could suggest has been introduced to give completeness and permanence to the work...". Alexandra Dock closed in 1983 but was reopened by ABP in July 1991.

Alexandra Dock, Hull
Valentine`s Series not p/u

Alexandra Dock, Hull
"C.P." series East Park Studio, Hull No.209
p/u 1919
"...*it will take us about 40 hours from here to Southampton...*" presumably the journey was by sea.

Coal awaiting shipment at Alexander (sic) Docks, Hull H & B Ry.
This offical Hull & Barnsley Railway postcard sent by the Hull & Barnsley Railway, Mineral Department, Alexandra Docks, Hull in June 1907 to the Dalton Main Collieries Ltd., Rotherham advises that "...*the matter is being given special attention*"! Surely all these coal wagons cannot have been lost!

Coal awaiting shipment, at Alexander Docks, Hull.   H & B. Ry.

17

Alexandra Dock, Hull.

Alexandra Dock., Hull
PPC "Philco" Series No.4189 not p/u
This postcard dates from the First World War period as it is
printed on the back with the information "Passed for publication
by Press Bureau 15/3/17", so presumably no state secrets are
shown!

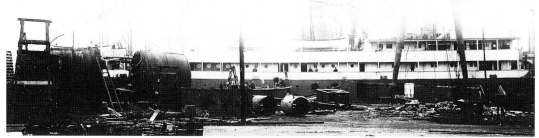

Earle`s Crane

r/p not p/u

When Earle's shipyard, at Victoria Dock, closed in 1932-3, ending large-scale shipbuilding in the city, the famous landmark crane was sold, along with all the tools, machinery and equipment, shipped out to the Far East and re-erected in Kowloon.

Hull.   New Riverside, Quay.

New Riverside Quay, Hull

The Milton Fac-Simile" Series No.54
Woolstone Bros., London EC
not p/u

Riverside Quay of 1907, built mainly of wood, was destroyed during the Second World War Blitz, but was rebuilt in concrete after the war and opened on 12 May 1959.

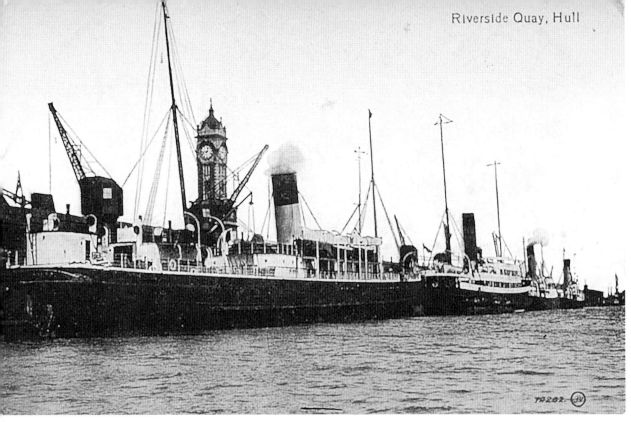

Riverside Quay, Hull
Published by W British Made
not p/u
The clock tower survived the Blitz damage but was later demolished.

King George V Dock, Hull
P/c not p/u by W.A.R. Co. 7-47
King George Dock was opened in 1914.

3. RAILWAYS

General View Railway Goods Station Neptune Street, Hull H .& B. Ry.
An official Hull & Barnsley Railay postcard, postally used in 1907.
"Thought I would let you know I am not going to get home on Monday but will let you know when".
Neptune Street was the Hull & Barnsley Railway`s main goods station handling traffic for the docks west of the River Hull and general merchandise for the city centre. Electric cranes installed new in 1906 can be seen.

Sculcoates Junction signal box, Hull & Barnsley Railway

This signal box controlled the Hull & Barnsley Railway's Sculcoates goods station and coal yard, which until recently was the last rail-served coal yard in Hull. The signal box closed on 4 October 1954.

[PW]

Paragon Station, Hull

"Aldwych" series, W.H.S. & S. London. 3769 Printed in Germany

The Royal Station Hotel, fronting the south end of Brook Street, later Ferensway. Seen on the left demolition of property in Regent`s Terrace, Anlaby Road, possibly including the Hull & East Riding Club, subsequently rebuilt on the south side of Anlaby Road to allow the extension of Brook Street southwards to link with Anlaby Road.

This site was later occupied by the Theatre de Luxe cinema, later the Cecil Cinema.

4. HESSLE ROAD

Hessle Road, Hull

Hessle Road, a relatively recent development; it was turn-piked only in 1825; became associated later in the 19th Century with the fishing industry, with many of the terraced houses in courts and streets off the south side off Hessle Road occupied by trawlermen, their families and other occupations linked to the fishing industry. Fishing smacks from Brixham and Ramsgate arrived in Hull in the 1830s and 1840s, and in 1845 there were twenty nine smacks operating out of Hull, whilst by 1878 this number had increased dramatically to 386. At first the fishing smacks used the Humber but gradually moved into a corner of the Humber Dock and by 1851 when Dock dues were reduced all used the dock, where the 'Billingsgate' fish market was held. The fishing fleet increased in size and moved first to Albert Dock which opened in 1869 and eventually St. Andrew`s Dock built as a permanent base for the fishing fleet in 1883. This concentrated the fishing industry in an isolated position at the west end of the town, and Hessle Road became the heart of the fishing community. This view of Hessle Road looking west, shows on the left, at the corner of Madeley Street, the Primitive Methodist chapel of 1880-1 by William Freeman and on the right, at the corner of Coltman Street, the Public Benefit Boot & Shoe Company`s shop of 1898 by William Alfred Gelder. Although the chapel is now sadly empty the former schoolroom at the rear is occupied by the Northern Theatre Company. The former Public Benefit shop has recently been splendidly restored by Premier Workwear.

The Fishermans Memorial, Hull
W&S not p/u

Hessle Road, Hull

Another view of Hessle Road, this time looking east, with the
Hessle Road Congregational chapel of 1875-7 seen on the right.

Fishermans Memorial Statue

r/p no publisher p/u 1906

The statue, depicting Captain George Smith of the 'Crane', by Hull sculptor Albert Leake was erected in 1905, commissioned by the Royal Antediluvian Order of Buffaloes (R.A.O.B.). Although the inscription on the plinth states that it was unveiled by Lord Nunburnholme this was actually done by John Watt, a local magistrate. The statue, now listed Grade II, at the junction of Hessle Road and South Boulevard, has recently been restored. Note that contrary to a popular myth which has built up locally, the figure is not holding up a fish in his hand. The graves of the three victims, Walter Whelpton died later, can still be seen in Western Cemetery off Chanterlands Avenue. Part of one of the damaged trawlers, showing the shot holes, is on display in the Town Docks Museum.

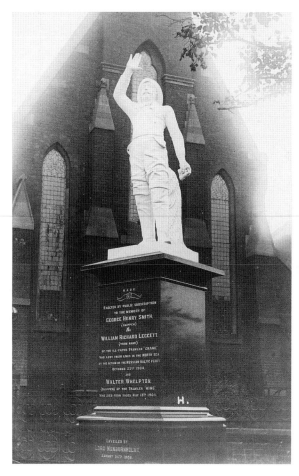

Hull Trawlers Shot at by Russians
not p/u

Russian Outrage, Damaged Trawler, S.T. 'Moulmein' and Crew (No.1)
not p/u

Russian Outrage, Damaged Trawler, S.T. "Moulmein" and Crew. (No. 1)

Russian·Outrage, Damaged Trawlers, "Moulmein" and "Mino" (No. 3)

Russian Outrage, Damaged Trawlers, 'Moulmein' and 'Mino' (No.3)
p/u 1906

On the night of 21 October 1904 the Russian Baltic squadron fired on a fleet of Hull trawlers in the apparent belief that they were Japanese torpedo boats. Six trawlers were hit, one The Crane, sank, two men were killed, and others injured, one dying later from injuries. The Dogger Bank Incident or Russian Outrage as it became known caused an international incident. These postcards probably form part of a set of six.

Both *The Graphic and The Illustrated London News* produced supplements illustrating the attack by the Russian gunboats on the Hull trawlers, the damage caused and the principal characters involved. National and local postcard publishers quickly produced sets of cards and individual views, showing an artist's reconstruction of the 'incident', the damaged trawlers 'Moulmein' and 'Mino' back in dock, the funeral procession for Captain George Smith and William Leggett, the victims' graves in Western Cemetery and the Fishermens Memorial statue.

5. CHURCHES AND CHAPELS

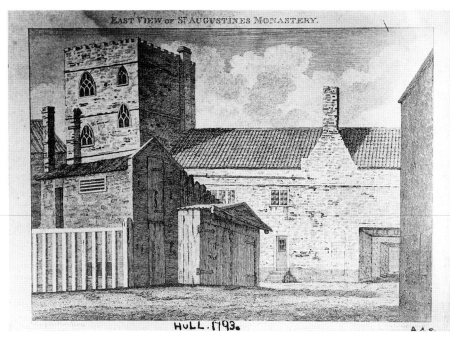

East View of St Augustine`s Monastery

This 'A&S' (perhaps Abba & Sons?) photographic postcard reproduces the well-known view of "East View of St. Augustine`s Monastery". But is it what it purports to be?

The site of the Augustinian or Blackfriars Friary (not monastery) is bounded to the south by the medieval Monkgate, now Blackfriargate, to the west by the medieval Marketgate, now Market Place, to the north by the present King William House multi-storey car-park and to the east by High Street; this site was excavated in 1994 prior to redevelopment of the site. The Friary was in existence from 1317 to 1540. This view, by Benjamin Gale, which is from Tickell`s History of Hull, 1796, is traditionally supposed to show the then recently demolished remains of the friary described as "...near the Guildhall, a square tower with gothic windows, six stories high, and a long range of buildings running north and south which had been converted into a public house known as the Tiger Inn...". However Tickell was the first writer to suggest that the tower was associated with the Augustinian Friary, earlier historians not having made reference to it. Finds from the archaeological "dig" will be displayed in the new Hull & East Riding Museum in High Street and the detailed report of the recent excavations by the Humber Archaeology Partnership is eagerly awaited.

Charter House Hull

An FO, Frank Overton, real photographic postcard shows the 18th Century Charterhouse buildings in Charterhouse Lane. The Hospital or Almshouse has its origins in the Carthusian Priory founded in the late 14th Century by Michael de la Pole which stood on a nearby site to the north of the walled medieval town. The hospital was rebuilt in its present form in 1778-80, probably to the designs of Joseph Hargrave. The De la Pole`s coat of arms can be seen over the semi-circular domed porch entrance to the chapel.

Charlotte Street

This real photographic postcard shows No.70 Charlotte Street. James S. Smithson, pork butcher, is listed in the 1899 directory; and Mrs. Mona Smithson, pork butcher, in 1916.

On the right can be seen part of the Bethel Methodist New Connexion Chapel. This chapel originally built in 1799 was altered in 1875 when the front was given an Italianate appearance with a porticoed entrance. The chapel which had seating for 800 was destroyed by bombing in 1941. Its site is now a road junction at the corner of Freetown Way, George Street and Wilberforce Drive. Charlotte Street was part of the new road layout, including Savile Street, George Street, Charlotte Street, North Street and Bridge Street, created by the Hull Dock Company following the construction in 1774-8 of The Dock, later Old Dock, Queen`s Dock and now Queen`s Gardens.

Ebeneezer Primitive Methodist Chapel, Spring Bank

This large chapel built in 1877-8 at a cost of £8,060, to the designs of Hull architect William Freeman, was of white brick with stone dressings with a "Greco-Italian front capped with pyramids", or what might be described as Italianate with French Renaissance detailing. It had seating for 1,000; the chapel had closed by August 1944 and was demolished in 1976. The site is now the yard of a vehicle hire firm near the corner of Middleton Street. Ebeneezer was only one of the many large 19th Century churches and chapels on Spring Bank, mostly now demolished. Others included Jubilee, the Presbyterian Church, St. Jude`s Anglican church; and the New Jerusalem or Swedenborgian church which survives as a second hand furniture warehouse.

Beverley Road Baptist Church

This splendid real-photograph 'F.O.' postcard by local photographer Frank Overton not p/u.

Overton had studios at 85 Prospect Street and later at 20 Savile Street and in Newbegin, Hornsea

c1905-1915??

This former Baptist church dates from 1904 and together with its large adjoining halls, one of which is earlier and formed the original church, are now Grade II listed. The architect of the church was George Baines & Son of London. The unique design, in the Free Perpendicular Gothic style, is of red brick, panelled with flint nodules, and a spired octagonal turret. The interior of this church, now the Trafalgar Street Evangelical church, has a false hammer-beam roof with traceried spandrels, and an all-round traceried wooden gallery with rounded corners.

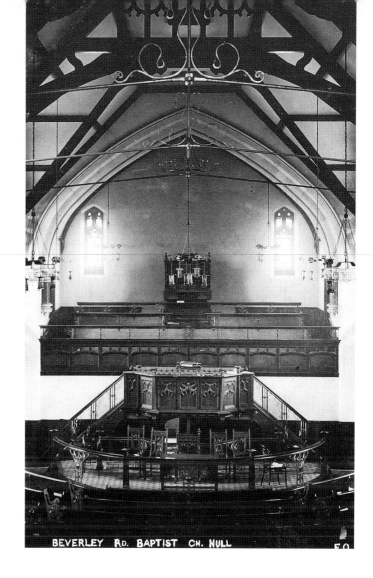

BEVERLEY RD. BAPTIST CH. NULL

Guide Troop, Ebeneezer PM Chapel

The large 19th Century non-Conformist chapels provided the focus of social activity and entertainment for their congregations; Ebeneezer seemed to have been particularly active in this way and there exists a large number of postcards showing events such as concerts and pageants, and groups of Boys Brigade, Scouts and Girl Guides.

Interior St. James`s Church, Hull

A.C. Garton Studios, Porter Street Post Office, Hull and Withernsea not p/u

St. James`s Anglican church in St. James Square, Lister Street off the south side of Hessle Road was consecrated in 1831. It was built as a chapel-of-ease to Holy Trinity church to serve the expanding population of the Potteries area in English Town to the south of Hessle Road, and was assigned its own district in 1874. The church, designed by J.A. Hansom (of Hansom-cab fame) and E. Welch, was a Church Commissioners church, being funded partly by the Government and partly by the Hull Corporation. It had seating for 1,000; major alterations were made in 1866, 1871 and again in 1931 when the galleries were removed. The church closed at Easter in 1957 and was demolished in 1959; the site is now a grassed area in the middle of the Square off the east side of Alfred Street.

West Street Memorial Church

Now known as Perth Street chapel, this shows the 1931 building prior to the removal of its stone pediment. The original 'tin tabernacle', the first church on the site, can be seen, which survives, minus its gothic steeple, as the present church hall. The chapel was developed by the congregation from the West Street Primitive Methodist Chapel, in Mill Street, which was the first Primitive building in Hull of 1819. There are numerous 'foundation stones' incorporated into the chapel at the corner of Chanterlands Avenue and Perth Street which record these connections with West Street.

St. Paul`s Church, Hull

St. Paul`s Anglican church, in St. Paul`s Street, Sculcoates was consecrated in 1847. The church, built of stone in the Early English style, was designed by William Hey Dykes with seating for 950, and alterations were made in 1877 by Smith & Broderick. The steeple was removed in 1958 and the church demolished in 1976. A new church was built on almost the same site; although the former vicarage survives.

The photograph is by G.E. Thompson, who had studios at No.220 Holderness Road in the early years of the century and later moved to No.34 George Street. He produced a number of good real photographic postcards.

[JM]

Kingston Chapel, Witham, Hull

The Kingston Wesley Chapel, in Witham was built at a cost of £8,000 in 1841 to the designs of James Simpson. The Greek Revival style chapel was of brick but with an impressive stone facade with a large pediment supported on four massive Ionic pillars. It had seating for 1,750 by 1881, was damaged by bombing in 1941 and was later demolished. Its site on the north side of Witham near the corner of Holborn Street is now a petrol filling station and car showroom. It is difficult to imagine that an area like Witham, now devoted almost entirely to the motor car, was once a densely populated area requiring the provision of large places of worship like Kingston.

KINGSTON CHAPEL, WITHAM, HULL

Lowgate & St. Mary`s Church, Hull. 'EGRO' Hull

E. Grocock, a second-hand dealer whose pile of 'junk' outside his shop in Wellington Terrace, on Beverley Road was a familar local sight, published many 'home-made' postcards in the 1930s, often reproducing old views. Edward Grocock, plumber is listed at No.109 Beverley Road in the 1937 directory; he was still there in the 1950s.

St. Mary`s church, one of only two medieval churches in Hull, first mentioned in 1327 and described as "new built" in 1333, was a chapel of ease of North Ferriby until the 17th Century. The tower collapsed in 1518 demolishing the west end of the church and the present tower dates from the rebuilding of 1697. Although built of brick with stone dressings the tower was encased in Earle`s Roman cement in 1826. The church was heavily restored in 1861-2 by Sir George Gilbert Scott, when the base of the tower was pierced with a stone-vaulted walkway. The churchyard is now paved with graveslabs removed during Scott`s restoration. The drinking fountain seen here at the entrance to the churchyard from Lowgate has been removed.

Wesley Hall

Overton`s Photo Postcards. Agent G.M. Coult, 133 Spring Bank

p/u 1904

The Wesley Chapel in Humber Street was built in 1832-3, designed by William Sissons of Hull, at a cost of £3,600. The chapel was remodelled in 1887 and became the Wesley Hall, which closed in 1905, and the building became a fruit auction room. The building was demolished following Second World War Blitz damage, and a modern fruit warehouse, Nos.66-8 Humber Street now occupies the site.

WESLEY HALL   HULL

Anlaby Road, Hull

p/u 1903

The church of St. Matthew designed by Adams & Kelly was built in 1870 at a cost of £7,000. 'Pevsner' comments "a tough church but a convinced one"; its spire is an important Hull landmark, there being no other surviving Victorian churches in Hull with spires.

LABY ROAD, HULL.

HOLY TRINITY CHURCH, HULL.
Photographed after the Air Raid, June 6th., 1915, by T. Moorby, 13 Spring Street, Hull.

Holy Trinity Church, Hull
Photographed after the Air Raid, June 6th, 1915 by T. Moorby, 13 Spring Street

The most terrifying aspect of the First World War to those on the 'Home Front' was the air-raids made on the towns and cities near the East Coast by Zeppelins, vast rigid air ships some 500 feet long and 40 feet wide. Hull`s first air raid was at midnight on Sunday 6 June 1915 when a Zeppelin spent twenty minutes over Hull and dropped a number of incendiary and high explosive bombs on the Old Town and Drypool areas of the city, killing twenty five and injuring about 100 people. The second raid was on 5 March 1916 when two Zeppelins hovered over the city for an hour and dropped bombs causing extensive damage in the Queen Street and Collier Street areas, the glass roof of Paragon railway station being destroyed. Seventeen people died and 60 were injured. An attempted raid on 5 April 1916 was not successful but another on 8 August killed nine and injured 20. Photographs of damaged property, from the Hull Daily News and Hull Weekly News were issued as a booklet, showing scenes of destruction in Campbell Street, Church Street in Drypool, Bright Street off Holderness Road and Holy Trinity Church and the Market Place. This postcard shows Edwin Davis` store at the corner of South Church Side and Market Place destroyed, but Holy Trinity Church escaped serious damage.

Interior St. Mark`s Hull

St. Mark`s Street

The postcard of St. Mark`s Street by M. Barnard, Marine Photographer and Post Card Publisher, Hull, is postally used in 1907. Note that the truncated steeple of St. Mark`s church can be seen. This Anglican church was consecrated in 1844 to serve a district of Sutton, together with the extra-parochial area of Garrison Side, in The Groves. The church, which had seating for 1,115, was designed by the architect H.F. Lockwood of Hull, and was altered in 1881 by local architects Smith & Broderick. The top twenty-five feet of the spire were lost in a gale in 1863, the spire later being partly removed and the lantern rebuilt. The church was badly damaged in the Second World War Blitz, closed in 1948 and demolished ten years later. Its exact site is now lost in a timber yard off the north side of St. Mark`s Street.

All Saint's Church, Hull.

22309. JV.

All Saints Church, Hull

All Saints Anglican church was consecrated in 1869 and immediately replaced St. Mary`s, Air Street, as the parish church of Sculcoates, the area to the north of the Old Town where much of Hull`s expansion took place in the 19th Century. The church was built to a design by G.E. Street of London the leading Victorian church architect; the tower by local architect Samuel Musgrave being added in 1883. The church, with seating for 1,100 was in turn replaced as parish church of Sculcoates by St. Stephen the Martyr on Spring Bank, originally the rebuilt Jubilee Methodist chapel, in 1972. All Saints closed and was demolished in 1974, a campaign to preserve the tower being unsuccessful. Its site is now occupied by housing in Cavendish Square off Margaret Street.

St. Giles Church, Marfleet

c1938 photo by Jerome`s

This church, built in 1884 to a design by J.T. Webster of Hedon, replaced the earlier church rebuilt in 1793 to the design of George Pycock of Hull. Some memorials from the 18th Century church survive in the present church which still stands, somewhat isolated in the centre of Marfleet, now surrounded by industry. It is difficult to imagine that Marfleet was a separate community, older than Hull itself; a church at Marfleet was first mentioned in c1217; as Hull`s industrial expansion, including the eastern docks, in the 19th Century has destroyed almost all the rural and agricultural character of Marfleet, although one 18th Century farmhouse survives next to the church.

All Saints Church, Hull

George includes rather a saucy message to Lucy on this view of the interior of All Saints *"...still very hot Don`t be surprised if you see me minus trousers..."*! He`s already told her on this 1911 postcard that he`s *"...in the pink"*

Hawthorn Gypsy choir, Hull

Other postcards exist showing this choir about which I know very little. I think they were probably associated with the Norman Memorial Chapel of 1905, in Hawthorn Avenue at the corner of Anlaby Road.

Holy Trinity Church, Hull

The west end of Holy Trinity Church is seen here in this view from the corner of King Street and South Church Side. The open market area in the foreground was formerly part of the church-yard. Often described as one of the largest (by area) English parish churches, Holy Trinity was established as a chapel of ease for Hessle parish, perhaps in 1285 and did not become a parish church until 1661. The transepts and lowest stages of the crossing tower are of brick, this being the earliest major case of the use of brick for a church in England. Major restorations were carried out in 1841-5 by H.F. Lockwood, in 1859-72 by Sir George Gilbert Scott and by F.S. Brodrick in 1906. A major restoration appeal has recently been announced.

Altar of Our Lady St. Charles R.C. Church Hull

W&S Hull p/u 1905

St. Charles Borromeo, in Jarratt Street, of 1828-9 is by John
Earle junior. The church was widened and altered internally and
externally in 1835 by J.J. Scholes and in 1894 much altered by
Smith, Brodrick & Lowther. The stuccoed five-bay front with
rusticated quoins is largely of 1835. 'Pevsner' comments "The
restrained exterior does not prepare one for the striking Baroque
interior". The colourful interior including dome, Lady chapel,
and narrow aisles with arcades of paired Ionic columns is by
Immenkamp, with plasterwork by Geo. Jackson & Son, London.
St. Charles is listed Grade II.

6. SPORT

Hull & East Riding Hockey Club 1905-6
This real-photographic card not p/u but dated 1908 includes one M.A. Birtles

Carlton Thursday A.F.C. 1913-14
This real-photographic card by Duncan, Photo, 15 Anlaby Road is not p/u and includes no details of names of the team members

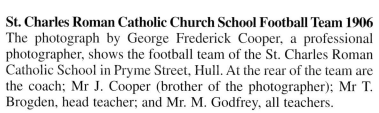

Holderness Road Prims

The photograh by Crown Photo Co., Durham Street, Hull shows what I take to be the football team from the Holderness Road, Bright Street, Primitive Methodist chapel.

St. Charles Roman Catholic Church School Football Team 1906

The photograph by George Frederick Cooper, a professional photographer, shows the football team of the St. Charles Roman Catholic School in Pryme Street, Hull. At the rear of the team are the coach; Mr J. Cooper (brother of the photographer); Mr T. Brogden, head teacher; and Mr. M. Godfrey, all teachers.

Cricket at Newland Cottage Homes

PB1160 not p/u

This shows Hull Zingari Cricket Club, on the cricket field behind the school at Newland Orphan Homes on Cottingham Road, which they occupied from 1900 to 1910.

Hull Municipal Technical College football team 1933-4

There exist many real photograhic postcards; like this one published by 'Swain, Photographer, Hessle, E. Yorks'; which show amateur sports teams. Some are captioned with the name of the team, others are not. If one is lucky, the name of the team can be ascertained from the caption written on the football, in this case 'H.M.T.C. 1933-4'. However no-one has thought to record the names of the team members on the back of the photograph, so some remain 'unknown'. I have identified Dimishky(?) second from left, top row, Ingleby second from right top row, and on the front row from the left Maurice Potter, Mowforth and Andrews in the centre. The location is Hull City`s Anlaby Road ground next to the Cricket Circle.

[HC]

Hull Railway Clerks Cricket Club, 1919
[MU]

Hull Kingston Rovers N.U.F.C. 1919-20
This postcard shows the Rovers Northern Union Football Club team of 1919-20, probably at Craven Park. Those identified include back row top left T. McGiever and top right F. Bielby; middle row left to right W. Clark, W. Bradshaw, A. Moore (captain), two unidentified; front row bottom left R. Rees, next to him G. Austin. The real photographic card is by Duncan, Photo., 15 Anlaby Road, Hull.
[MU]

Hull Zingari Cricket Club 1905

The cricket club, now based at Hull & East Riding Athletic Club on Chanterlands Avenue, has just celebrated its Centenary.
[MU]

Hull City AFC

Hull City AFC Company Limited came into being on 28 June 1904 and this real photographic card by Garside shows the Hull City team on the left and Notts. County players before the Tigers` first match as a professional club in September 1904. The location is Boulevard where the team first played before moving to Anlaby Road.
[MP]

44

7. MILITARY

Londesborough Barracks, Londesborough Street

The 4th East Yorks. Regiment at the Londesborough Street Barracks p/c not p/u by R.T. Watson, photographer, Hull. Londesborough Barracks were built at a cost of £2,200 in 1864 as the Rifle Barracks by the 1st East Yorkshire Rifle Volunteers; the street itself and the barracks taking their name that year from their Honorary Colonel, Lord Londesborough. There were other military influences in this area, which in the mid 19th Century would have been on the edge of the town providing large open spaces for barracks and parade grounds. Wenlock Street being named in 1889 for the 2nd Baron Wenlock who was Honorary Colonel of the 2nd East Riding of Yorkshire Volunteer Artillery; and nearby in Park Street the Artillery barracks, originally erected in 1870 for the purpose of the Working Mens Art and Industrial Exhibition, bought in 1871 by the 2nd East York Artillery Corps. The site, along with the adjoining Corporation Field was later acquired by Northern Dairies as their transport depot. This site is now empty and awaiting redevelopment; although the Londesborough Barracks are still in military use.

South African War Memorial
SW

The Heroes of the British Submarine E13, 1915

Funeral Procession in Hull of Submarine E13 Heroes
Photo Garton, Hull

19 Aug 1915 *"You could nearly walk on the heads of the people. I did not go but those who saw it said it was a sight. I see funerals enough for I am sure every time I go down in the car we meet 2 or 3, some times more. There are two burial places and the jews` is at the street end".*

Hull was the scene of one of the most moving funeral processions of the war, when the victims of the E13 disaster were brought ashore, in August 1915. The E13 submarine had left England on 15 August for deployment in the Baltic. On the 18th it ran aground in the narrow waters between Denmark and Sweden, whilst sailing on the surface. A German destroyer opened fire on her, badly damaging the submarine before being stopped by Danish M.T.B`s. Whilst transferring survivors to Danish ships the submarine blew up. Fifteen men died in the incident which caused world-wide outrage as it occurred in neutral Danish Waters; Denmark later gained an official apology from Germany. The bodies of the victims arrived in Hull for transport to their home towns on 27 August, and a funeral procession passed through a packed city centre on the 28th, en route for Paragon Station, Hull. Of the dead, one was a local man, Herbert Staples, an engine room artificer from Grimsby, his body being taken home across the Humber by tug. The Hull Times gave an account of the crew`s last moments based on eye-witness reports. It described this as "one of the most stirring deeds of heroism in British and Naval history". According to Danish fishermen "Suddenly we saw a torpedo rush through the water, miss and explode on the sand bottom. Again we heard a short sharp word of command and immediately the men got up and formed into a line on deck with crossed arms facing the enemy`s guns, immovable as statues and looking death in the face without moving a muscle. They were brave men these English". A postcard was published reproducing an artist`s view of the 'incident' itself and numerous photographic cards appeared showing the funeral procession. 'In Memoriam' cards were also produced listing the names of "The victims of the E13, Torpedoed by the German navy on the Danish Coast. August 23rd 1915".

John Cunningham, V.C. East Yorks. Regt.

H. Miles, Publisher, 23 Brook St.

The Hull Brigade was formed in the First World War following the Lord Lieutenant of East Yorkshire, Lord Nunburnholme`s instruction of 29 August 1914 to raise a local battalion of men. In only eleven weeks enough men enlisted to form four infantry battalions, 4,000 men in all which together made up Hull`s own infantry brigade, the 92nd. These battalions were given unofficial names reflecting the men`s backgrounds, which were kept after they became part of the East Yorkshire Regiment (E.Y.R.) The 1st Hull Battalion "Commercials" formed the 10th Battalion E.Y.R.; the 2nd Hull Battalion "Tradesmen" formed the 11th Battalion E.Y.R.; the 3rd Hull Battalion "Sportsmen and Athletes" became the 12th battalion E.Y.R.; and the 4th Hull Battalion "Pals or T`Others" formed the 13th Battalion E.Y.R. The Hull Brigade saw action in all the major offensives, but its blackest hour came on 3 May 1917, when as part of the Arras offensive the brigade went "over the top" at the village of Oppy, north east of Arras. In fierce fighting around the village and Oppy Wood the brigade lost more men on this one day than at any other time during the war. The attack failed and the final casualties totalled 326. Private John Cunningham of the 12th (S.) Battalion East Yorkshire Regiment was awarded the Victoria Cross for most conspicuous bravery and resource during operations at Hebuterne Sector, France on 13th November, 1916. This postcard by H. Miles, publisher, 23 Brook Street was produced to commemorate Cunningham's valour. Miles specialised in producing postcards of the many war memorials or street shrines erected in local streets listing casualties of the area. Only four of these street shrines still remain in situ, in Marfleet Lane, Sharp Street, Dansom Lane and Eton Street.

JOHN CUNNINGHAM, V.C.
EAST YORKS. REGT.

H. Miles, Publisher, 23, Brook St.   *Copyright.*

Unveiling of Soldiers Memorial November 5 1904
The moment before the flag is removed and the statue is
unveiled with a gun salute is depicted here in this PB real
photographic card.
[JC]

We are going to spend a short time in the Country. Will you join us?

'Trekkers' setting off at night to take shelter in the countryside, from the First World War 'Blitz' on Hull when bombs were dropped from Zeppelins. Note the factory 'buzzers' acting as air-raid sirens. Part of the message on this card reads "*We have not had another visit from Aunt Maria but still expecting her...*". Is this perhaps a private code referring to the Zeppelin raids? The postcard was sold by 'Clark`s Postcard Stores, 21 Anlaby Road, Hull'. Postcards were produced showing the damage caused by bombs dropped from Zeppelins and damaged property.

Empire Sunday Parade 1912

Dated 8 June 1912, this real photographic card published by Duncan, 15 Anlaby Road & the Studio, Clarendon Street, Hull shows the Central Hall Company of The National Reserve marching proudly along Park Street over the railway bridge towards Anlaby Road on their way to church. The terraced houses in the background survive, but the former Hull & East Riding College of 1866, later the Hull High School for Girls, has recently been demolished and new houses, Belgrave Mansions, built on the site. One wonders how many of these men marched off to War, never to return, within two years. Park Street developed from the mid 19th Century being "tastefully laid out" with "elegant houses", replacing muddy country lanes alongside sewers and a ropery, known variously as Pest House Lane, Dog Kennel Lane and Cut Throat Lane. More elegant names for parts of the street, as it later developed with large houses and terraces, were College Lane and Elm Tree Avenue. There were a number of educational institutions in the area in addition to the Hull & East Riding College, including the original Hull College, of 1837, at the corner of Spring Bank, replaced by Minerva Terrace; and the Reverend Henry William Kemp`s 'Thanet House Academy' founded in the mid 1850s, the origins of the Port of Hull Society`s orphanage, which forms the basis for the present Park Street Centre of Hull College.
[JC]

8. ANOTHER LOOK AT
THE OLD TOWN

Town Hall, Hull

p/u 1906

The old Guildhall of the town stood at the south end of the Market Place, but when this became dilapidated a house in Lowgate was leased intially for three years from 1805, subsequently bought and retained as a Town Hall until the building seen on this postcard view was constructed on the same site in the 1860s. The foundation stone was laid on 9 October 1862 and the building opened, at a cost of £50,000 on 25 January 1866. The Town Hall, designed by local architect Cuthbert Brodrick, was demolished in 1912, following the construction of the first phase of the present Guildhall, and the Guildhall was extended eastwards to occupy the site of the Town Hall fronting Lowgate.

Town Hall, Hull

Town Hall, Hull

not p/u

Although the Victorian Town Hall was demolished when the eastern end of the present Guildhall was constructed between 1912 and 1916 much of the building materials still exist. Some are in Pearson Park; in addition to the well-known cupola, various stones around the serpentine lake are from the Town Hall, whilst parts were taken to Brantingham and used to build the village`s war memorial of 1922, described as "elephantine" by 'Pevsner'. Other parts of the Town Hall, including various urns, adorn the tops of gatepiers to large houses in Brantingham and there is still more at Brantinghamthorpe Hall.

New Law Courts, Hull

This Milton "Fac-Simile Sunset" Series No.240 postcard by Woolstone Bros., London EC, p/u 1913 shows the new law courts, part of the Guildhall, shortly after construction. Note that the second, eastern, phase of the Guildhall has not yet been constructed and the rear of the original Town Hall can be seen at the corner of Lowgate. On the right is the Police Station at the corner of Alfred Gelder Street and Parliament Street.

New Law Courts, Hull.

Whitefriargate, Hull

This Valentine & Sons Ltd., "Silveresque" postcard bears the message *"A view of one of the Shopping centres in Hull. The shops down here were not damaged by air raids"*. On the right the British Home Stores Nos. 63-67 Whitefriargate, a classic Moderne-style stuccoed front of 1934 by A.L. Farman with suntrap windows. The shop was later extended one bay to the west or left in the same style in 1956-7.

WHITEFRIARGATE, HULL.

Whitefriargate

The medieval Aldgate which included Silver Street and Scale Lane as well as Whitefriargate, took its later name from the Carmelite or White Friars whose friary, established in the 13th Century, was on the south side of the street. Later Trinity House occupied this site.

Whitefriargate was, along with Trinity House Lane, the first of the city centre streets to be pedestrianised in the 1970s.

WHITEFRIARGATE, HULL.

Humber Street

A splendid real photograhic PB card here showing the eastern end of the north side of Humber Street with the entrance to Little Lane seen on the left. On the extreme left, one of the Old Town`s many 'Lost Pubs' at No. 46 Humber Street, the former Labour in Vain (1813-1867), New Bridge Inn (1872-1876) and Tiger No.6 (1879-1892). Humber Street, originally the Fore and Back Ropery formed the southern boundary of medieval Hull, with the waters of the Humber washing against the brick walls along the southern side of the street. Land south of Humber Street was reclaimed from the Humber in the early 19th Century when the spoil dug out during the creation of New (later Humber) Dock in 1807, was dumped on the foreshore and the southern end of Queen Street, Wellington Street, Nelson Street and Pier Street laid out. Little Lane gave access to the heart of the Old Town and the Market Place via Blackfriargate from the ferry landing place near the mouth of the Old Harbour, at the east end of Humber Street and south end of High Street.

Triumphal Arch, Whitefriargate Royal Visit to Hull May 12th 1903

p/u 27 June 1903

The event or rather events marked by the erection of this triumphal arch in Whitefriargate, were the laying of the foundation stone of the City Hall and the unveiling of the statue of Queen Victoria in Queen Victoria Square. The then Prince of Wales, later King George V, unveiled the statue of Queen Victoria on 12 May 1903, followed by the laying of the foundation stone of the City Hall by the Princess of Wales, later Queen Mary. Building triumphal arches, perhaps copied from the Arc De Triomph in Paris and the Marble Arch in London, themselves inspired by the discovery during the Renaissance of the ruins of classical arches built for the returning heroes of the Roman Empire, usually for visits by Royalty became something of a tradition in the country in the Victorian period. In Hull the specific historical reference seems to have been to the Beverley Gate and there were at least five separate arches built at this site (not actually the exact site of the gate, as shown by the later archaeological excavation) in Whitefriargate. In other parts of the country local vernacular building materials were used; bales of cotton and cotton spinning machinery in Preston, boats and nets in Hastings, firemen's ladders in Runcorn for the opening of the Manchester Ship Canal, and in Northwich the centre of the Cheshire salt making and chemical industry, arches were made from blocks of salt and salt barrels. The Hull examples all seem to have been made of wood perhaps covered with painted canvas, and marked Royal visits, those in 1854, 1869 and 1884 all involved arches in Whitefriargate; and the launch of the cruiser HMS Endymion built by Earle`s in 1891 when an arch was built across Hedon Road.

TRIUMPHAL ARCH, WHITEFRIARGATE.
ROYAL VISIT TO HULL, MAY 12TH, 1903.

53

9. SPRING BANK

Spring Bank, Hull

p/u 1904

The line of Spring Bank forms part of the ancient boundary between Sculcoates to the north and Myton, later the combined parishes of Holy Trinity and St. Mary`s to the south. A survey of Sculcoates dated 1691 shows the alignment as 'Darringham Bank'. The street itself has as its origins a narrow lane running alongside the open Spring Ditch, or Dyke, which brought fresh water to Hull from Spring Head to the west. The dyke was later arched over, a line of lime trees planted along it and a footpath, originally only on the south side laid out as a 'promenade'. As early as 1803 building sites in Spring Street were advertised "in a pleasant country situation", but the street was not fully developed until the late 1830s when it was still described as "in the country yet near the town". The first property built fronting Spring Bank itself was Spring Row at the eastern end, part of this property survives between Spring Street and Hall Street. Elegant terraces such as Carlton Terrace, Minerva Terrace, Brunswick Terrace and Belgrave Terrace were built in the 1840s and '50s and by 1891 Brown`s Guide was able to describe Spring Bank as "This pleasing suburban road". Sadly the avenue of lime trees has gone as have the Zoological Gardens (1840-1863), many of the large 19th Century chapels have been demolished and a petrol filling station has replaced the former Hull Seamen's and General Orphan Asylum, latterly Government Buildings. However many of the original mid to late 19th Century terrace houses survive, the pub names preserve memories of the Zoological Gardens (Polar Bear, Tap & Spile the former Eagle, and Old Zoological) and Botanical Gardens (Botanic); and Spring Bank is now a Conservation Area.

SPRING BANK, HULL

10. FIRMS` OUTINGS

Hammonds Pic-nic to Matlock July 1911
[JC]

Hammonds has its origins in a small drapery & hosiery shop near North Bridge started by H.W. Hammond, opened in 1821, which after forty years trading moved to Osborne Street where it remained until 1916 when the well-known department store in Paragon Square and Jameson Street was opened. The store with its distinctive domed roof was bombed in 1941 and the present large department store opened in 1952. Following the sale of the business by the Powell family in the early 1970s the name of the shop was changed to Binns, but the familiar Hammonds name was restored in 1989.

E.C. Jubb`s Picnic Welton Dale June 1907

"Here is a puzzle for you, can you find me...? " asks Daisy, the sender of this card, to her friend Minne Rennard of Jane`s Place, Francis Street West, Hull. Mr. and Mrs. Jubb are in the centre of this group of the firm`s employees on their annual outing. Jubb`s was a large department store on Beverley Road near the corner of Fountain Road. Edwin Charles Jubb, draper is listed at No.4 Beverley Road Arcade, between Providence Row and Somerscales Street, in the 1892 directory and the shop later (for example in the 1916 directory) moved to No.142 Beverley Road, next to the National cinema.

Another 'works outing'

Photograph here by Duncan, Photo, 15 Anlaby Road, Hull; could they be employees of Owbridge`s? There are other photographs in this series, one showing people wearing 'silly hats', of which one bears the name Owbridge`s. W.T. Owbridge manufactured Owbridge`s Lung Tonic, "The Mighty Healer" at The Laboratory in Osborne Street. The Lung tonic was reputed to have "... a power over diseases hitherto unknown in medicine" and could cure severe attacks of bronchitis, bad coughs, lung disease and weakness, severe colds and loss of voice, weak chests, consumption; the diseases, once the Lung Tonic had been taken would "disappear as if by magic..."! The front of the Owbridge`s manufactory in Osborne Street, with its distinctive clock 'tower', survives incorporated into a new development of flats. Could this be a race meeting, perhaps on Beverley Westwood?
[JC]

11. HOUSE AND SHOP PORTRAITS

Gentlemens' Saloon. MARCUS, 23, Witham. Hull.

Gentlemen`s Saloon MARCUS, 23 Witham, Hull
What a strange subject for a postcard; the interior of a small hairdresser`s shop in Witham. This postcard by Lilywhite Ltd., Triangle, Yorks, is presumably an advertising card.

Wilcock`s Cash Stores
Wilcock`s Cash Stores Grocers & Provision Merchants not p/u c1920. This shop, at the corner of Derwent Street, was one of three shops owned by Wilcock`s.
[P]

Kimberley Street

Unidentified baby, who, the message dated 1907 informs us *"...has not been well today"* stands, at the door of this house in Kimberley Street, off Argyle Street, Hull. Kimberley Street was named in 1889 when the South African 'gold rush' was at its peak; the houses were demolished in the 1970s.

Unidentified house

I have not yet identified the location of the Victorian terraced house portrayed in this 1907 postally used postcard. Can you?

C.T. Empson, Fish & Ice Merchant

The children standing outside their father`s 'Fried Fish & Potatoes' shop in Argyle Streeet, Hull are George Empson (born c1908) and his sister Hilda. The photograph is dated c1908, and is a splendid example of the 'shop-front portrait' only usually found in family albums. Might this have been one of the earliest fish 'n' chip shops in Hull? Notice that Mr. Empson`s business had branches at Portland Street, Francis Street, North Street, Alexandra Road and Clarendon Street. Property in Argyle Street was demolished in the 1970's.

A. Evison
Albert Evison, fruiterer & greengrocer, No.74 Church Street Drypool. The proprietors stand in the doorway of their small greengrocer`s shop in Drypool in this 1920s 'shop portrait'. Much of the property in the 'village' centre of Drypool was demolished in the 'slum-clearances' of the 1930s.

G. Coleman, shopkeeper, Hull Road, Anlaby
Although this real photographic card, not postally used, but possibly dated c1907, is actually of Anlaby, it is Hull Road, Anlaby, and I cannot resist including it as another splendid example of the shop-front portrait genre of real photographic cards found in family albums. Sadly no other information has survived with this postcard although it seems reasonable to assume that the couple posing in the shop doorway are the proprietors, Mr. & Mrs. Coleman.

12. LIBRARIES

Beverley Road Free Library, Hull
The Wrench Series Nr.11790 'Printed in Saxony'
This card, postally used in 1904 refers, as so many cards of this period do, to the postcard collecting craze itself. *"Thanks for card. Trust you will like this one as well. I like the one you sent me."*
The Northern Branch Library of 1894 by architect H.A. Cheers of Twickenham in the late Gothic style with a squat castellated tower with pyramidal roof and mullioned and transomed windows, is now a Grade II listed building. The interior has a splendid hammerbeam roof.

Carnegie Library, Hull
PB 858 p/u 1905
The Carnegie Library at the entrance to West Park on Anlaby Road was designed in 1905 by the city architect Jospeh H. Hirst. Its central feature is the half-timbered two-storey octagon with a pyramidal roof; there is a sloping tiled roof to the verandah running along the front of the main building and to the left a half-timbered single-storey wing. The library is listed Grade II.

New Central Library, Hull

New Central Library, Hull.

Reliable Series

The Central Library in Albion Street is of 1900-1 by the London architect J.S. Gibson. It is of five bays, red brick with stone bands and dressing. The central bay is of ashlar and projects, with a recessed entrance porch, large round-arched window and pedimented gable. There is an octagonal corner tower, the upper part projecting above the roof has Ionic columns with semi-circular pediments and is supported by a dome. The former reference library is now the local studies library and retains most of the original features including a decorated plaster barrel-vaulted ceiling. The back of the card which is undivided, has had a pencil line drawn in to allow the message to be written on the same side as the address, which prior to 1902 was not permitted. The card was probably issued in 1901, note that the library is called 'new', and used the following year, 1902.

Public Library and Baths, Holderness Road, Hull

PUBLIC LIBRARY AND BATHS, HOLDERNESS RD, HULL.

Raphael Tuck & Sons' OILETTE regd. Postcard 7144
not p/u

The James Reckitt Library, Holderness Road of 1888-9 by W. Alfred Gelder was Hull's first public library paid for by James Reckitt and presented to the town. It is in the Gothic style of red brick with Ancaster and Howley Park stone dressings, of two storeys, seven bays with central three-storey tower, pointed arched windows to the first floor and an arched entrance with oriel window above. The adjoining Holderness Road Baths of 1897-8, is probably by Joseph H. Hirst. It has what 'Pevsner' describes as a "showy facade" of red and yellow brick bands with terracotta decoration. It has a wonderfully ornate tiled entrance hall.

13. PEOPLE

Sailors` Orphan Homes, Newland, Hull
The Wrench Series No.1306 Printed in Saxony
This undivided back p/c is postally used in 1902.

Newland Orphan Homes - sailor boys
The Newland Homes, originally Newland Orphan Homes was established by the Port of Hull Society following their move from the Park Street orphanage (now the Park Street Centre of Hull College) in the late 1890s. The Homes of 1896-9 are designed by W.H. Bingley. Substantial individual grey brick houses, named after benefactors, are grouped round a large open green, with a school, now St. Nicholas primary school, at the north end. Part of the extensive site stretching north to Inglemire Avenue was later sold, and forms part of the Inglemire campus of the University of Lincoln and Humberside. The Newland Homes are now run by the Sailors Families Society.

Sailors' Orphan Homes, Newland.   Hull.

'Cakes and Angels'

Cakes and Angels seems an appropriate title for this unidentified view of a group of little girls dresed up in their party best frocks. And won`t their Mums be cross when they arrive home with chocolate icing and cake crumbs (they are surely angel cakes?) down the fronts of their best dresses! The only clue to a possible location for this event, perhaps a chapel anniversary?, is the photographer`s name, Storey & Hall, 45 George Street, Hull. The card is not postally used, so cannot be dated and sadly no-one thought to write names, date or occasion on the back. I urge you all to check your own family photograph collections and record as much information as you can now before the information is lost forever. [JC]

Telephonists, Mytongate Telephone Exchange

Photograph dated September 1921

The first telephone exchange in Hull was converted by the Post Office from an existing telegraph office in about 1880. The National Telephone Company opened a rival exchange in Bowlalley Lane in 1890, and later in Mytongate and Fish Street including the former Fish Street Congregational chapel acquired in 1898. In 1895 the P.O. had 52 subscribers and the N.T.C. 742. Hull Corporation obtained a licence to provide a telephone service in 1902 and opened an exchange in the former Trippett baths in 1904, later taking over the National Telephone Company`s system. Mytongate became the main corporation telephone offices, which were damaged by bombing in 1941. The two central exchanges were replaced in 1964 by Telephone House in Carr Lane. Kingston Communications remains the only municipally owned telephone system in the country.

Hull Fair 1935

Chicken Joe

Joe Barak ran a 'Bingo' stall at Hull Fair from the 1920s until the 1960s and became a well-known and well-loved local character at the annual fair. Many people recall buying the winning 'raffle' ticket (presumably if you did not win you did not remember!), the numbers chosen by a spinning arm rotating on three large wheels, later replaced by flashing electric lights, and winning the star prize of a large brown paper carrier bag-full of groceries, topped by what, in retrospect always seemed an enormous, chicken, then something of a luxury. Hull Fair postcards are eagerly sought after by collectors and nearly always command high prices at the specialist collectors shops and postcard fairs.

Chicken Joe the Man You All Know

14. THE VICTORIAN AND EDWARDIAN CITY CENTRE/ CITY HALL/ DOCK OFFICES

The City Hall, Hull

Bromby`s Views of Hull

The City Hall, in Queen Victoria Square is an imposing Edwardian Baroque building designed by City Architect Joseph H. Hirst. The foundation stone was laid in May 1903 and the building constructed in five phases, completed in 1909/10. There are many postcards showing the City Hall in various stages of construction and progress of the building work can be used to date a non postally used card.

The City Hall, Hull
p/u 1913

The City Hall, Hull.

Prudential Buildings

J.D. Series 110

The Prudential building of c1903 by Alfred Waterhouse & Son was badly damaged by high explosive bombs dropped on the centre of Hull during the night of 7 May 1941 during one of the heaviest raids of the war. Fifteen people sheltering in the basement of the building were killed. The following day after removal of the bodies, the tower which was all that remained of the building, was demolished. Its site is marked by a plaque in front of the Paragon Street/King Edward Street corner of Queen`s House .

[MP]

Monument and Bridge and Dock Offices, Hull

p/u 1904

The Dock Offices, of 1867-71, designed by Christopher G. Wray, were built on a triangular island site at the centre of the 'Town Docks' between Queen`s Dock and Prince`s Dock. Although now one of the main features of Queen Victoria Square the Venetian Renaissance style building with its prominent three domes, was originally in Junction Street and actually pre-dates the creation of the Square. The Grade II listed building, the third dock office to be built by the Hull Dock company, was acquired by Hull City Council in 1968 and converted into the Town Docks Museum, Hull`s maritime museum, which opened in 1975.

MONUMENT AND BRIDGE AND DOCK OFFICES, HULL.

Monument Bridge, Hull
W.J. Wellsted & Son Photographers Hull
p/u 1906

Wilberforce Monument & Dock Offices, Hull
Reliable Series p/u 1903
The Wilberforce Monument "a colossal fluted Doric column, on a square pedestal surmounted by a statue of 'the great philanthropist' standing on a small circular pedestal above the capital". The first stone of the monument was laid on 1 August 1834, the date of the abolition of slavery in the colonies of the British Empire. William Wilberforce who was born in Hull in 1759, was a leading figure in the campaign for the prohibition of slavery. The cost of the monument was £1,250 raised by public subscription. The monument was dismantled over a few weeks from April 1935 and re-erected at the east end of Queen's Gardens, its present position, by the beginning of August that same year. Local builder Tarran carried out the work as an advertisement for his firm. A red square in the road, outside Monument Buildings, marked the exact original position of the monument in what was St. John's Street, but would now be described as the south-east corner of Queen Victoria Square, until the pedestrianisation of Queen Victoria Square in c1988. A metal plaque in the red-brick paving next to the pedestrian crossing now marks the spot and records "Original site of the Monument to William Wilberforce M.P. for Hull then Yorkshire and slavery abolitionist. Erected in 1834 the monument was moved to the east end of Queens Gardens in 1935".

Wilberforce Monument & Dock Offices, Hull.   RELIABLE W&S SERIES

Monument Bridge, Hull

Published by W British Made

Valentine`s 65640

Although at first glance these four cards bottom left p67, top and bottom p68, and this page appear to show a very similar scene, there are a number of years separating the three photographs and various significant changes can be traced. The earlier view (page 67) sold by F.W. Martindale, 67 Carr Lane, Hull, although postally used in 1904, is probably at least one year earlier. Property bounded by St. John`s Street, Engine Street, Waterworks Street and Junction Street has been demolished, to create Queen Victoria Square. The statue of Queen Victoria has been unveiled and the foundation stone of the new City Hall laid, although little, if any, building appears to have taken place. The Prudential Building of c1903 by Alfred Waterhouse & Son, at the corner of Waterworks Street and King Edward Street, can be seen to the right of the Wilberforce Monument. On the right the Dock Offices (the third built by the Dock Company) with their unique triple domes, with beyond, the Dock Company`s stables, now The Warren.

The second view, postally used in 1906, shows that work on the construction of the City Hall has progressed with the first phase, the eastern end including the dome, having been completed. On the left can be seen the tall chimney of the electric tram system`s electricity generating station in Osborne Street, over the roof of St. John`s church. The church of St. John was the first to be erected outside the confines of the old walled town and was built at a cost of £4,600 at the sole expense of the Rev. Thomas Dykes in 1791. It was bought by Thomas Ferens in 1917 and demolished c1924 to provide the site for the Ferens Art Gallery.

The fourth, later, view by national postcard publishers Valentines, shows the completed City Hall with the roof of the art gallery, or Victoria Galleries now The Mortimer Suite visible. On the left is Monument Buildings of 1908 now incorporated into the Prince`s Quay shopping centre. The view is probably of c1910.

Monument Bridge, Hull.

Wilberforce Monument, Hull
Published by A.J. Wellsted, 367 Spring Bank W., Hull

Temporary Bridge, Hull P.B.960
Note that Parrish & Berry have had difficulties spelling 'temporary'!

The rebuilding of Whitefriargate or Monument Bridge, linking the Old Town with the Victorian and Edwardian town centre to the west, was necessitated by the construction of Alfred Gelder Street in 1901-3 and whilst the main bridge was rebuilt this temporary bridge was provided. The bridge ran from the corner of New Cross Street and what is now Queen`s Dock Avenue to the west of the lock-pit between Queen`s Dock seen on the right of this view, and Prince`s Dock off to the left. Its eastern end, in the foreground of this view, is at the corner of Junction Place (the present alignment is the pavement in front of the Burton`s shop windows) and what was South Side Queen`s, or Old, Dock, now Guildhall Road and the new Alfred Gelder Street. The bridge was for pedestrians and horse-drawn traffic only, not trams. The new Whitefriargate Bridge, colloquially 'Monument Bridge' was opened on Wednesday 9 May 1906. However trams did not use the new bridge immediately, the tram service eventually being resumed on 31 May 1906, and 'TH' trams were using the bridge by 29 July 1907. The 'P' service could then terminate in Queen Victoria Square and passengers no longer had to walk over the bridge. In the background can be seen the former Dock Company`s stables, now the Probation offices and The Warren resource centre, and on the extreme right a wooden bell pole behind the temporary newsagent`s kiosk. The bell would be rung to warn traffic and pedestrians of the impending closure of the bridge to allow shipping to enter the lock-pit between the two docks. A similar restored bell-post has been re-erected next to the entrance to the marina at the Humber Dock lock-pit.

Monument Bridge, Hull

National Series M & L., Ltd. not p/u

Try telling a stranger to Hull that you will meet them in town at 'Monument Bridge' and they will be lost! Because of course the 'Monument', Wilberforce Monument was removed in 1935 and the 'Bridge'; originally Junction Bridge (after Junction Dock, of 1829, later Prince`s Dock) later Whitefriargate or colloquially, Monument Bridge, which was completely rebuilt in 1905 to accommodate the electric trams, was demolished in 1932. Parts of the foundations of the 1905 bridge were exposed during the 1988 excavations of the Beverley Gate and have been preserved in the 'amphitheatre' surrounding the foundations of Beverley Gate and the 14th Century brick town walls. "Meet you at Monument Bridge!"

Monument Bridge, Hull.

Royal Institution
p/u 1904
[P]

Wilberforce Monument & Dock Offices from Princes Dock
(coloured p/c) p/u 1907
This view shows St. John`s church, the building at corner of King Edward Street/Savile Street, Yorkshire Penny Bank, Dock Offices, Wilberforce Monument, and Hull Brewery chimney. The Hull Brewery chimney, a familar sight on the skyline of many similar postcards was constructed in 1903 by Coates of Barton on Humber. It was designed by Freeman Sons & Gaskell, replacing two smaller stacks from the original 1867 brewery actually known after the firm`s founders 'Gleadow' and 'Dibb'. The chimney was demolished following the sale of the Silvester Street Anchor Brewery by Mansfield Brewery, who had purchased North Country, in 1989 and conversion of the Grade II listed brewery into The Maltings business centre.

Wilberforce. Monument & Dock Offices from Princes Dock.

15. KING EDWARD STREET

King Edward Street, Hull

This view shows the east side of King Edward Street

"This is a popular and most busy part here, the streets are pretty wide but could do with widening yet more. Only go here on Sunday when togged up like Lords` sons. A favourite place for the casual young lady and partner, full of shops displaying fine gowns, furs and other dainty articles. Ha Ha! Frank".

King Edward Street

King Edward Street was constructed from c1901 as part of the town centre improvement schemes which also involved the building of Jameson Street, and slightly later the creation of Queen Victoria Square. "Slum" property was cleared away and wide streeets more suited for the new electric tram system were opened.

16. THE PIER

Corporation Pier
p/u 1905
paddle steamer 'Doncaster'

Corporation Pier.   Hull.

Victoria Pier, Hull
WR&S Reliable series - undivided back
This postcard actually shows Minerva Pier in the foreground
with Victoria Pier in the background.

Victoria Pier, Hull.

The Humber, Looking East, Hull
Valentine`s series 22652 not p/u
Sammy`s Point is on extreme left at
the mouth of the Old Harbour, River
Hull. The paddle tug 'Sam' enters
the mouth of the Old Harbour.

Ferryboat Pier, Hull
Published for Stewart & Woolf,
London EC Printed in Saxony
Series 284. Sold by F.W.
Martindale, 67 Carr Lane, Hull
PS Grimsby(?)

Hull Victoria Pier
Peacock Brand p/u May 24th 1904
Queen Victoria`s Birthday.

HULL.   Victoria Pier.

The Horse Wash, Victoria Pier, Hull
Bromby`s Views of Hull
Known colloquially as "`oss wash".

THE HORSE WASH
VICTORIA PIER, HULL

Victoria Pier, Hull.

Victoria Pier, Hull
W.H.S. & S. Humber Series, Hull p/u in 1907
*"Dear Mary We expect to go here today, I saw
some men launch a ship near the Humber..."*

Victoria Pier, Hull
Valentine`s Series not p/u

Victoria Pier, Hull

Valentine's Series

31846

17. HOLDERNESS ROAD and
EAST HULL

Holderness Road
"Humber" Series
Prior to the construction of the direct Hull to Hedon turnpike road in the 1830s, Holderness Road, via Wyton and Preston, was the main route into and out of Holderness from Hull. Most of the suburban developments along Holderness Road took place in the 19th Century.

Holderness Road.

Hull, Holderness Road

This card; showing the Brunswick Wesleyan chapel, built in 1877 at a cost of £4,500. The architect of this Italianate style chapel with seating for 920, was Samuel Musgrave; is overprinted on the back with an advertisement for 'Merrill`s Celebrated ICES, CUSTARD & BLANC-MANGE POWDERS Sample & full particulars post free, 1/-, G.P. Merrills 46 & 55 Walker Street, Hull'.

21904   Hull. Holderness Road.

East Park Flower Beds, Hull.

East Park Flower Beds, Hull

This Boots Cash Chemists "Pelham" Series postcard p/u 1912 shows a rather uninspiring scene in East Park. But where is the elevated position from which the photograph is made?

JAMES RECKITT AVENUE, HULL.

James Reckitt Avenue, Hull

Raphael Tuck & Sons' "Real Photograph" Postcard is postally used in 1944. James Reckitt Avenue is named after James Reckitt (1833-1924) the youngest son of Isaac Reckitt who came to Hull in 1840 and founded the business of Reckitt & Sons Ltd., of which James became director and chairman. He was made a baronet in 1894, the year he moved to Swanland Manor. James Reckitt was the originator of the Garden Village, to which James Reckitt Avenue leads.

RECKITT & SONS LTD.

HEAD OFFICE AND KINGSTON WORKS, HULL, *from the Air.*

Reckitt & Sons Ltd., Head Office and Kingston Works, Hull from the Air

The photograph on this advertising postcard is by The Aircraft Manufacturing Co. Ltd., Hendon, N.W.9 The printed message on the card reads "An aerial view of the Head Office and Kingston works of Reckitt & Sons Ltd., at Hull, where Robin Starch, Reckitt`s Blue, Reckitt`s Tints, Zebra Grate Polish, Brasso Metal Polish, Silvo Plate Polish &c., &c., are made. Reckitt & Sons, Ltd., Hull. The Directors desire to remind Shareholders that they will be furthering the interests of the Company by purchasing any of the articles contained in this list all of which are manufactured by the Company". There follows a list of various Starches, Reckitt`s Paris Blue, Black Leads and Metal Polish including Brasso, Shinio, Bluebell, Mepo and Grate Paste.

The Garden Village, Hull

Publisher F.C. Hull

This locally published postcard shows the Village hall which was demolished following war damage. Garden Village was developed on the former grounds of Holderness House from 1907 onwards for Sir James Reckitt, a Quaker industrialist. The Garden Village designed by Percy T. Runton and William E. Barry was opened on 2 July 1908 and by 1913 over 500 houses had been built, largely although not exclusively for employees of Reckitt & Sons. The Oval, a large open green, the central feature of the village, is surrounded by tree-lined streets and avenues, the Shopping Centre, and the Club House both of 1909. There are also various groups of almshouses, the Juliette Reckitt Haven of Rest of 1911, the Frederick Reckitt Homes of Rest, 1912 and the Sir James Reckitt Village Haven of 1924. Garden Village was the first of Hull`s Conservation Areas.

THE GARDEN VILLAGE, HULL.

In the Garden Village, Hull

In The Garden Village, Hull

Valentine`s Series

Lover`s Walk can be seen alongside The Oval.

The Garden City, Hull W&S
Published by W.J. Wellsted &
Son, Photographers Hull

St. Mark`s Scouts in the Garden Village

This group of scouts belonged to the Incorporated Church Scout
Patrol who later joined the Baden Powell scouts. The message
spelled out by their semaphore flags, as they pose for their
portrait in the garden of a Garden Village house, reads "St.
Mark`s".

18. STATUES

Andrew Marvell Statue, Hull W&S Hull

Published by W.J. Wellsted & Son, Photographers, Hull
One of Hull`s many 'moving' statues. Andrew Marvell is seen here in his second position, after being removed from the Town Hall to the corner of Smeaton Street, George Street and Savile Street. The statue of "the incorruptible patriot" by Hull sculptor William Day Keyworth was later moved a few yards to the corner of Bond Street and George Street. It is now sited outside the former Grammar School, now William Gee School. In the background can be seen the Hull Savings Bank, at the corner of Smeaton Street, parts of which survive behind the modern frontage of the TSB at the corner of George Street and Bond Street.

Andrew Marvell Statue

Another splendid Parrish & Berry real photographic postcard, PB29, showing a different view of the poet`s statue with Wilson`s Corner and Savile House, the offices of Henry Wilson & Son Ltd., wine & spirit merchants, behind. The offices have been demolished, but the former retail premises of the spirit merchants survive as The Dram Shop public house.

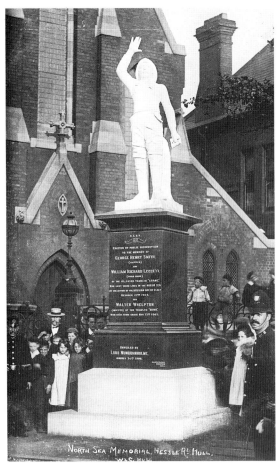

North Sea Memorial Hessle Road
W. J. Wellsted & Son, 20 Paragon Street, Hull not p/u

Wilberforce Memorial, Hull
KUH30
A 1950s photograph showing the Wilberforce Monument in the centre of College Circle at the east end of Queen`s Gardens. The road layout has since been altered with the creation of Wilberforce Drive, which has given some the mistaken belief that the monument has been moved twice. It was moved only once, from St. John`s Street ('Monument Bridge'), to its present position at the east end of Queen`s Gardens in 1935.

Wilberforce Memorial, Hull.   KUH30.

Soldiers Memorial Statue

p/u 1904

In the background, above the OXO and Nestlé Milk advertisements, can be seen the then newly rebuilt Waverley Hotel, now the Master`s Bar, at the corner of South Street and Jameson Street; and on on the left property in Temperance Street replaced during the construction of Jameson Street. This memorial to the men killed in the South African War "Erected by public subscription to the memory of the men of Hull who lost their lives during the South African War 1899. 1900. 1901. 1902" takes the form of a sculpted pair of soldiers on a pedestal. It was unveiled on 5 November 1904. The cost was £650.

Unveiling of Soldier`s Memorial Nov 5th 1904.
This PB card is postally used only three days later.

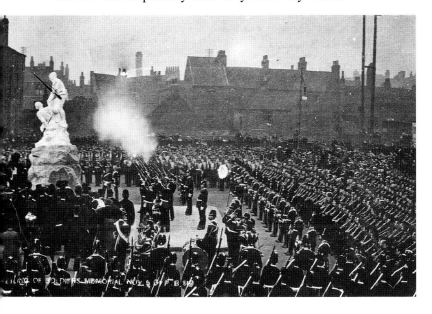

Soldiers Memorial Statue

Paragon Square property in the background includes the Commercial House commercial rooms and a beer retailer`s on the exteme left. Also seen is Meek`s Umbrella Manufacturer`s, listed in the 1907 directory at Nos.25-6 Paragon Street as James W. Meek, hairdresser and umbrella maker.

Unveiling of the Hull Cenotaph

The Hull Cenotaph in Paragon Square "Erected to the memory of the men of Kingston upon Hull who laid down their lives for their country in The Great War 1914-1918". Although this real photographic postcard, which is not postally used, has had the date of 1923 written on the front, it is likely that this date is incorrect and should be 1924. The cenotaph incorporates a date stone "laid by the Rt. Hon. The Lord Mayor of Hull, Councillor Charles Raine JP 8 November 1923" and it seems likely that this was a foundation stone. Minutes of the Hull City Council dated 26 September 1923 refer to drawings by the architect T. Harold Hughes, who had won a competition to design the memorial, and further minutes of the 8 December 1924 refer to the contractor being Quibell`s. The cenotaph was unveiled 20 September 1924. The inscription on the Portland stone monument, erected by public subscription, concludes "Their Name Liveth for Ever More".

19. AERIAL VIEWS

Hull, Old Town with Parish Church & Guildhall from The Air (2288)

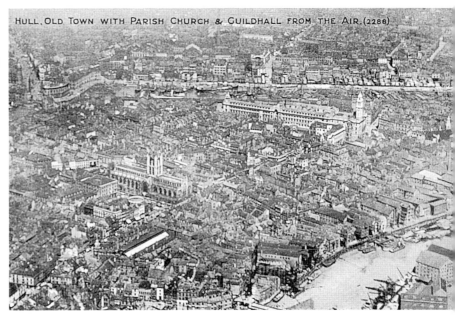

Aerial View of the Heart of Hull, King Edward Street, City Hall & Dock Offices (2289)

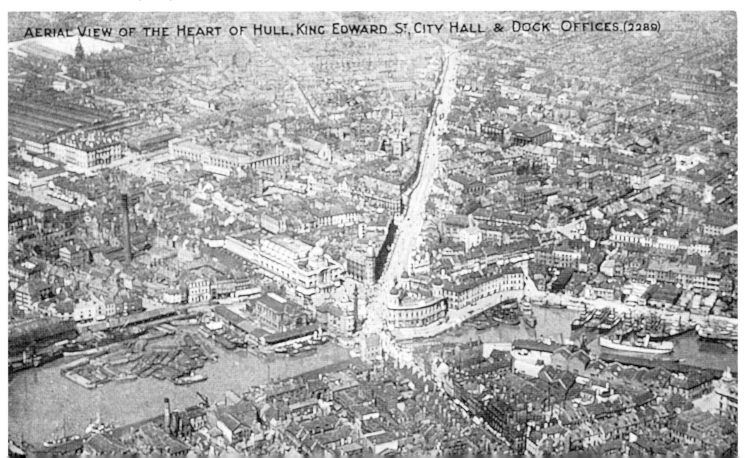

HULL, CORPORATION PIER, DOCKS & RIVER FROM THE AIR. (2240)

Hull, Corporation Pier, Docks & River From The Air (2240)

Hull, Aerial View of Pier, Docks & River (2241)

Part of a set of six aerial view postcards, these fascinating views provide much of interest to consider. Perhaps the main problem is to date the views accurately. Although the postcards themselves were probably published in the 1930s, the 'logos' on the back of these printed postcards by Photochrom Co. Ltd., London & Tunbridge Wells, by arrangement with The Aircraft Manufacturing Co. Ltd., show a biplane. It is possible that the photographs themselves; could they have been made from an airship?; may have been made in the early 1920s or even the late 'teens. The fixed dating features I have indentified so far include an 'earliest possible' date of post-1915 - see the site at the corner of South Church Side and Market Place where a fairground carousel occupies the site of the Ewin Davis' store demolished by bombs dropped by Zeppelins in 1915. The 'latest possible' date, 1924, is provided by the still in-situ St John the Evangelist church in St. John`s Street. The church was demolished after this date to create the site for the construction of the Ferens Art Gallery opened in 1927. Can anyone provide a more precise date than circa post-1915 to´circa pre-1924 for these views?

HULL, AERIAL VIEW OF PIER, DOCKS & RIVER (2241)

20. ANLABY ROAD

Anlaby Road, Hull

527 no publisher, not p/u

The Tower Cinema of 1914, and the Art College of 1904 are prominent on this view of the town end of Anlaby Road looking towards Regent`s Terrace and Carr Lane from the corner of Midland Street. Anlaby Road historically forms the main route out of Hull to the west. There should be a sign reading "Rest of the World This Way!" at the town end.

Anlaby Road, Hull

A Valentine`s series postcard p/u 1911

The message realates to Harry`s night-time cycle ride from Scarborough to Hull. He writes to tell *Mother & All at Home* that he *"Arrived safe last night but very tired... the wind was in my face most of the way home and wouldn`t let me get on at all... I punctured about Beverley and had to keep pumping up. Fortunately it was a very fine night..."*

Boulevard

Boulevard is seen here looking north in this view from near the corner of Gordon Street on the left. Note the fountain in the circus at the the junction of Cholmley Street.

The land on which this "fine public promenade" was laid out belonged mainly to H.S. Constable, John Saner, W.H. Broadley and the Charterhouse Estate. A report in the Hull Times 4 June 1870 referred to "Another proposed Public Improvement for Hull". Mr Joseph Fox Sharpe, Surveyor to the Local Board of Health, had laid before the Town`s Improvement Committee an "admirable plan" for connecting the Humber Bank with the Hessle and Anlaby Roads a line of streets eighty feet wide as a public promenade. A row of lime trees would be planted within the footways so as to form an avenue 40 feet wide, with a carriageway in the centre. The line of this promenade would also be used to drain the area of St. John`s and Newland by continuing the line northwards across the North Eastern Railway`s land to join up with Spring Bank, and the Princess bank (Prince`s Avenue). Mr Sharpe`s project was received with "great favour" by the town`s Improvement Committee, and although they were "not disposed to advocate the carrying out of every new thing that is proposed to be done at the public expense" they believed that the cost of £7,000 would be "money... surely well invested..." There was some opposition to the proposal, Alderman Jameson objecting and suggesting that £2,000 would be a more apporopriate sum, and Mr Willows objected believing that the money would be better spent on a park. However a plan signed by Thomas Witty, Chairman of the Town`s Improvement Committee and J. Fox Sharpe, surveyor to the Local Board dated 21 April 1871, shows the "Plan for laying out land for houses fronting the Boulevard" which with some modifications formed the basis for the present appearance of the Boulevard. In general though the mainly terraced houses are more modest than those originally proposed and perhaps Sydenham House built as a doctor`s surgery in 1876 is the only individual house to be built in accordance with the original proposals, with a few others on the west side at the north end of the Boulevard. Shepherdson`s Guide of 1875 was able to record that [the Boulevard is] "...a very wide roadway planted with trees, the foot paths are broad, and at different parts there are convenient seats. About midway there is a large circular space with a colossal fountain in the centre...". By 1876 there were eight residents including the vicar of St. Matthews church, Robert Shaw an oil merchant, George Appleyard an ironmonger and Edward Elam a wine & spirit merchant. From the beginning of the 20th Century Boulevard became the favoured place of residence of those associated with the fishing industry, for example in 1907 there were increasing numbers of fish merchants, and fish dealers in the street and in 1916 occupations listed there included skipper, master mariner, marine surveyor, lighter owner, pilot, marine engineer, superintendent shipwright, engineer, fish salesman, mercantile marine officer, fish buyer, fish curer, tug owner, boiler maker, engine fitter, ship`s cook, hoistman, checker, mate, Custom officer, sailmaker, fisherman, shipwright, capstan man, stevedore, sailor, trimmer and fourteen fish merchants. The decorative cast iron fountain, similar in design to those placed later in the Avenues, was removed following a traffic accident c1930. 'Pevsner' comments "The street has plenty of large late 19th Century terraced housing with good details but it did not fulfil its early promise...". Boulevard is now a Conservation Area, the Conservation Areas: A Review report commenting "The unique origin of the Boulevard, its survival as a wide tree-lined avenue, together with many distinctive buildings and spaces, all contribute to its character...".

21. BEVERLEY ROAD

Prospect Street, Hull

p/u 1904

Prospect Street, originally part of Beverley Road is seen here in this coloured printed card. Bladon`s Bon Marché is on the left at the corner of North Street whilst in the centre can be seen the chimneys and windmill tower of 'Blundell`s Corner'. The present-day Prospect Street sadly retains little of architectural interest. Prospect Street marks the ancient boundary between Sculcoates on the east, right and Myton on the west, left.

Royal Infirmary, Hull

PB518 p/u 1905

[P]

The Infirmary opened in a house in George Street in 1782 and in 1784 moved to purpose-built premises on the Beverley Road, now Prospect Street, seen here. The Hull General Infirmary was designed by George Pycock of Hull, and was later altered by H.F. Lockwood in 1842. There were further extensions in the 1850s and 1860s and by 1865 the hospital had 150 beds. Further extensions took place in 1873 and 1885 and in 1884 the name changed to the Royal Infirmary. The new Hull Royal Infirmary on Anlaby Road was opened in 1966, the Prospect Street buildings being demolished and the Prospect Centre shopping centre built on the site.

ROYAL INFIRMARY, HULL, P. B 518.

Hull, Beverley Road

Raphael Tuck & Sons` "Town and City" Series 2022-Hull not p/u

The corner of College Street and Kingston Cottage is on the right behind the delivery cart in this view of Beverley Road looking north from near Trafalgar Street and on the left, Scarborough Terrace. Beverley Road Wesleyan Chapel is in the centre left beyond York Parade. The whole length of Beverley Road, as far as Newland, now forms the Beverley Road Conservation area. What a shame most of the trees shown on this view have not survived. Could they not be re-planted?

HULL. BEVERLEY ROAD.

The Last Old Horse Car

The Hull Street Tramway Company was incorporated in 1875, the Beverley Road route opened the same year. By 1899 the horse-trams were replaced by electric trams and Charles Dyson is seen here "putting up the shutters of the old horse system", flying the black flag to mark the end of an era, at the Temple Street depot, off Beverley Road, at Stepney in November 1899. On 5 July 1899 the electric tram system was inaugurated. The former horse-tram sheds in Temple Street were demolished in January 1985.

[P]

Grove Street

Another fine real photographic PB card showing Grove Street off the west side of Beverley Road at Stepney. A ten-foot at the end of the street leads into Pearson Park. I lived here at No.8 Grove Street when I first moved to Hull in 1968, and have always lived near the Park since. The north side (on the right) of Grove Street now forms part of the Pearson Park and Avenues Conservation Area. Note how neat and uniformed was the appearance of streets like this before they lost their decorative cast-iron railings. The 1876 directory records "here is a new road".

22. HOME-MADE CARDS

Most original Edwardian postcard album collections will include a few 'home' made' postcards; here are two, a portrait and a street scene.

"Bertha"
This delightful hand-drawn portrait of "Bertha" was sent by her friend Ethel to Miss Bertha Balding, 33 Marlborough Avenue, Prince`s Avenue, Hull in 1903.

Monument Bridge
A late 19th Century view by an unknown amateur artist, of Monument Bridge, probably copied from a photographic postcard, showing St. John`s church of 1792, the Hull & Sculcoates Dispensary of 1832, Wilberforce Monument of 1834-5, St. John`s Street, The Queen`s Hotel, Junction Street, the Dock Offices built 1867-71 and a horse-drawn tram crossing Whitefriargate or Monument Bridge. The view cannot be later than 1899 as this was the last year the Hull Street Tramways` horse-drawn trams operated.

23. PARKS

HULL. THE ARCH, EAST PARK.

Hull, The Arch, East Park

Raphael Tuck & Sons` "Glosso" Postcard Series 5543 "Hull"
SER.1

The printed caption to this postcard reads 'East Park The Arch.
This recreation ground which stands on the Holderness Road,
Hull, is one of the three extensive public parks which have been
opened in the town. It was thrown open to the public in 1887'
Thomas R. Ferens gave a site adjoining the park for a boating
lake, which was opened in 1913.

[JC]

Entrance and Almshouses, Pickering Park, Hull

postally used in 1913.

The Pickering Almshouses adjoining the attractive park gates are of 1909 design by Joseph H. Hirst.

Entrance and Almshouses, Pickering Park, Hull

West Park, Hull
H. Graham Glen, Wortley, Leeds Printed at the works in
Germany p/u 1905
The 31 acre West Park in Anlaby Road was opened in 1885.

West Park, Hull.

Rock Gardens Pickering Park, Hull

526

Pickering Park of 50 acres in Hessle 'High' Road was presented to the corporation by trawler owner Christopher Pickering and opened in 1911.

Rock Gardens, Pickering Park, Hull 526

West Park July 31st, 3 to 5

Hull Royal Infirmary, Newington Wards, Working Men`s Committee

Waterloo Prize Silver Band

Many postcards are seen like this with a concert programme printed on the back, the subject of the card often having no connection with the event advertised. In this case there is a link as it seems likely the Waterloo Prize Silver Band concert did take place in West Park. I am unclear whether these cards were handed out in advance as advertisements for the fund raising concerts or sold as programmes, the concert organiser presumably asking the printer to use up any unsold postcards to save costs.

POST 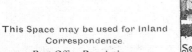 CARD

"Dainty" Series.

This Space may be used for Inland Correspondence.
Post Office Regulation.

The Address to be written here.

Hull Royal Infirmary, Newington Wards, Working Men's Committee.

West Park, July 31st, 3 to 5.

WATERLOO PRIZE SILVER BAND.

PROGRAMME

MARCH   "B.B. & C.F."   J. Ord. Hume
Overture " Cross of Jerusalem,"   M. Bleger
Selection   " Polinto,"   Donezetti
Air Varie   "Vesper Hymn,"   H. Round

Interval.

" War March of the Priest,"   Gounod
Selection " Gems of Welsh Melodies,"
                     J. Ord. Hume
Euphonium Solo   " Nazareth,"   Gounod
     (Soloist, Mr. T. Norman.)
Selection   " Norma,"   Bellini
     —GOD SAVE THE KING.—

24. PEARSON PARK AND THE AVENUES

Hull Prince`s Avenue
Postally used in 1906 this coloured printed card.
One of the Avenues` missing fountains is shown in this view of the circus at the junction of Blenheim Street, Prince`s Avenue and Park Grove.
[JC]

Westbourne Avenue
Where I used to live.

Prince`s Avenue, Hull

The Milton "Photolette" Series No.1109 Woolstone Bros. London EC. 2

A handsome boulevard, ornamented with trees and massive fountains, and lined on one side with elegant detached mansions, displaying almost every style of modern domestic architecture..." was how Brown`s Illustrated Guide described Prince`s Avenue in 1891. The alignment of Prince`s Avenue is the ancient boundary between Cottingham to the west and Sculcoates to the east and is shown on the 1691 Sculcoates Survey as 'The Kings Banckes'.Water-courses and drains were instrumental in determining the alignment of the muddy country lane known variously as Muck-peg lane, Newland Tofts Lane or Princess Bank, in the 19th Century, where there were a number of farms. The earliest developments, apart from farming in the area, were the establishment of the Hull General Cemetery Company`s cemetery at the corner of Darringham Bank (Spring Bank West) and Princess Bank (Prince`s Avenue) in 1847 and the building of two houses, now Nos.8/10 Prince`s Avenue as part of the Park Nursery in 1860. The opening of the "new Avenue... or Boulevard" took place in 1875 as part of David Parkinson Garbutt`s development of The Westbourne Park Estate, now known as 'The Avenues' and the press reported "... a considerable amount of success attending the ceremony... The neighbourhood was gay with bunting... a large marquee had been erected at the entrance to the Park.. flags were flying, the police band were sounding forth lively music and hundreds of people were assembled". 'The Avenues', Marlborough, Westbourne, Park and Victoria with Salisbury Street and Richmond Street continued to develop throughout the last quarter of the 19th Century, despite the developer Garbutt`s financial crisis ("a 'fall' from commercial grace"!) in 1883. 'The Avenues', a Conservation Area since 1974, continues to be an attractive area to live with what 'Pevsner' describes as "the most extensive area of Victorian middle-class housing in Hull... much of 'The Avenues' housing is standard late Victorian terraces but there is plenty of good detail and a range of individual designs". Of the six original fountains provided as part of Garbutt`s 'boulevard' design, only part of one, in Westbourne Avenue now survives.

[JC]

Princes Avenue, Hull.

Prince`s Avenue, Hull

Another wonderful PB real photographic card shows the entrance lodges and gates to the Hull General Cemetery at the corner of Spring Bank West and Prince`s Avenue, known colloquially as Spring Bank Cemetery. On the right is the Botanic Gardens railway station, originally known as Cemetery Gates. The Hull General Cemetery company formed in 1846 established its cemetery, now known colloquially as Spring Bank Cemetery, in 1847. By 1866 after extensions the cemetery covered about 20 acres. Hull City Council assumed ownership and responsibility for the cemetery, which had become overgrown and disused, in the 1970s and despite a campaign by the Friends of Spring Bank Cemetery, many of the gravestones were removed, the undergrowth cleared and trees and wildlife uprooted. The chapels and lodges shown in this view, designed by Hull architect Cuthbert Brodrick, were removed at various dates due to road widening at the corner of Prince`s Avenue and Spring Bank West and the gates and final buildings removed in the mid 1920s when the present shops with flats above at the corner were built.

Prince`s Avenue, Entrance to Pearson`s Park, Hull

The "D.F. & Co." Series Printed in England by Delittle, Fenwick & Co., York. Delittle Fenwick seemed to specialise in night-time scenes and as here postcards decorated with 'glitter'. This is one of the few views available of the Prince`s Avenue entrance to Pearson Park. Sadly both the ornate cast-iron gates and the fountain at the park entrance have been removed. The message to Nellie from Rose provides an intriguing glimpse into the life of someone who was presumably trapped in domestic service *"...Sorry I cannot accept your invitation for Sunday. I am like a caged bird I can`t get out. They have no-one to do for them if I was away. Hoping you will excuse this time. I shall come with the others tomorrow by way of a change. Don`t be offended by a postcard they are sometimes easier than a letter..."*
[JC]

Prince`s Avenue, Entrance to Pearson's Park, Hull

Prince Consort's Statue, Pearson Park, Hull

Pearson`s Park, Hull

A nice PB postcard showing children posing by the serpentine lake in Pearson Park. The bridge has been demolished, and many of the original Victorian features were removed in the 1950s.

[JC]

Pearson Park gateway
p/u 1906
The listed Grade II 'triumphal arch'
has recently been repaired.

Statue of Queen Victoria Pearson`s Park Hull
W&S Hull
One of my favourite postcards this charming view of a little girl in her sailor`s outfit poses with her pet dog next to the statue of Queen Victoria in Pearson`s Park. The statue, now listed Grade II, which dates from 1863 is by the Hull sculptor Thomas Earle.
[P]

Pearson`s Park, Hull
Another splendid real photographic PB card showing houses in the north-west corner of the park. Studley House, No.43 on the left, of 1862 by F.W. Hagen who designed many of the early houses in the Park, is now Grade II listed.

Pearson Park, Hull
This coloured Valentines card, postally used 1910, is the only postcard I have seen which shows the ornate cast-iron drinking fountain, which is now Grade II listed.

Pearson Park, Hull

Pearson`s Park, Hull

This view shows the Pearson Park entrance gateway from inside the park looking out into what is now known as Pearson Avenue, although originally was just 'entrance to park'. Dorchester Terrace is on the left. The gates themselves and the decorative features from the top of the 'triumphal arch' have been removed.

"Mam"
Ron Smith`s mum Olive Smith posing in front of the mermaid fountain in Pearson Park.

Nurse Camm`s Nursing Home, Westbourne Avenue/Salisbury Street, Hull
A policeman and a dog pose outside No.96 Westbourne Avenue. This is one of the "Gilbert Scott" houses in The Aveues, now International House.

25. INDUSTRY

Swan Flour Mills
r/p p/u 1906
[P]

Rose Downs & Thompson Ltd., Old Foundry, Hull
This advertising postcard showing an 'Aerial View of New Extension to Boiler and Welding Shop' was sent in 1948 to the British Electricity Authority Yorkshire Division at Sculcoates power station, with *"thanks for your esteemed order... which is having our careful attention"*. The aerial photograph not only shows the company`s premises in Cannon Street but, in the bottom right hand corner, the terminus of the Hull & Barnsley Railway.

Aerial View of New Extension to Boiler and Welding Shop

Invite your enquiries
for any class of

**STEEL
PLATEWORK**

•

TANKS

VESSELS
Jacketed or plain

HOPPERS

FABRICATED STEEL
COMPONENTS

ROSE, DOWNS & THOMPSON LTD.
Old Foundry, HULL

26. PUBS

George & Dragon, High Street

Builders Hotel, Cogan Street

The group seen posing in the doorway of this long demolished public house includes Charlie Bardsley, in the white apron, the bar-man; next to him Clara Bardsley, the land-lady who had the pub from before the First World War until c1938; and on the extreme right, holding the baby, Charlie`s wife Dora Bardsley.

Belgian Arms, Osborne Street
Members of the Belgian Ams Recreation club pose proudly in
the McMaster`s charabanc outside W.H. Bilton`s beer-house,
The Belgian Arms, on Sunday 12th August 1923.

Percy's York Commercial Hotel
Occupying three properties in Ocean Place, Anlaby Road, west of Midland Street, most of these buildings, dating perhaps from the 1830s, have been demolished for the 1920s re-building of the New York Hotel, although the shop seen on the extreme left survives now incorporated into the hotel.

Fishing club outing from Sportsman Hotel, Hedon Road

A pub outing, perhaps the fishing club, from the Sportsman Hotel, Hedon Road, in a Robert Winter`s horse-drawn charabanc can be seen here in this splendid real-photographic postcard, which is not postally-used, but may be of c1911. Property in the background includes Newton Terrace, James William Robins, coal & coke merchant at No.443 Hedon Road and Thomas K. Smithson, butcher at No.447 Hedon Road. The pub itself, The Sportsman Hotel at No.449 Hedon Road, just off to the right of this view, has quite recently re-opened.

Acknowledgements

Picture Credits
HC - Hull College
JC - Jean Clement collection
P - "Post The Past", Local History Unit, Hull College
MP - Mark Peacock collection
PG - Paul Gibson collection
JM - Josie Montgomery
MU - Mike Ulyatt collection
PW - Peter Wilkes
all other postcards are from the author`s collection

acknowledgements:- Peter Ablitt; Jack Allerston; J.H. Bardsley; Robert Barnard; Geoff Bell; André Brannan; Charles Brook; 'Miss Brown'; Martyn Chalk; Jean Clement; Mrs. E. Dixey; Peter Dorsett; Roy Dresser; John French; Paul Gibson; Alec Gill; Richard Hayton; Hull Stamp Shop; Mrs. Jefferson; Susan Johnston; Anne Ketchell; Tony Lewery; Local History Unit, Park Street Centre, Hull College; Josie Montgomery; David Neave; Park Street Centre Library, Hull College; Nicola Oehl; Mark Peacock; Simon Richardson; Michael A. Scrimshaw; Ron Smith; Robert Strafford; Alf Turner; Margaret Tuton; Ted Tuxworth; Michael E. Ulyatt; Gareth Watkins; David Wheldon; Peter Wilkes; Geoff Wilkinson; Roy Woodcock.

Bibliography

Images of Victorian Hull: F.S. Smith`s Drawings of the Old Town. C. Aldridge. Hull City Museums & Art Galleries and the Hutton Press, 1989; A History of the County of York East Riding Volume I The City of Kingston upon Hull. (ed.) K.J. Allison. Oxford University Press for the Institute of Historical Research, 1969; Barley Mash & Yeast: A History of the Hull Brewery Company 1782-1985. Robert Barnard. Local History Archives Unit, Hull College of Further Education and the Hutton Press Ltd., 1990; The Dram Shop: Henry Wilson & Son Ltd. Robert Barnard. Local History Unit, Hull College, 1996; Hull College: A History of Further Education in Hull. Robert Barnard. Hutton Press Ltd. and Hull College, 1996; The Slogan Postmarks of Kingston upon Hull. W. David C. Boddy and Martin Craven. Yorkshire Postal History Society, 1978; Handbook of Dates for Students of English History. (ed.) C.R. Cheney. Royal Historical Society, 1978; Postal History of Kingston upon Hull, Hedon and Holderness with historical information from the eleventh century to circa 1870. Martin T. Craven and John A. Fowler. Yorkshire Postal History Society, Sheffield, 1974; Iron and Steel Shipbuilding on The Humber: Earles of Hull 1853-1932. Arthur C. Credland. City of Kingston upon Hull Museums and Art Galleries, Bulletin No.15, 1982; Royal Rocks of Hull. R. Curry. Local History Unit, Hull College of Further Education and the Hutton Press Ltd., 1992; Revised List of Buildings of Special Architectural or Historic Interest: City of Kingston upon Hull. Department of National Heritage, 1994; Fares Please! The Twenty-Six Years` Reminiscences of a Tramwayman. C. Dyson. Hull, 1919 reprinted Malet Lambert Local History Reprints, Hull, Hull City A Complete Record 1904-1989. Chris Elton. Breedon Books, Derby, 1989; Beverley Gate: The Birthplace of the English Civil War. D. Evans and B. Sitch. Hull City Council and the Hutton Press Ltd., 1990; The Pen Pushers of High Street: A Centenary History of the Hull Zingari Cricket Club. D. Fairbank and M.E. Ulyatt. Hull Zingari Cricket Club, Hull, 1996; Hessle Road: A Photographer`s View of Hull`s Trawling Days. Alec Gill. Hutton Press Ltd., Cherry Burton, 1987; A History of Hull. Edward Gillett and Kenneth A. MacMahon. The University of Hull Press, Hull 1989; Collecting Picture Postcards. G. Godden. Phillimore Ltd., Chichester; A New Picture of Georgian Hull. Ivan and Elisabeth Hall. William Sessions Ltd., York and Hull Civic Society 1978/9; Last Orders Please! Index Edition: A Guide to the Lost Hotels, Inns, Taverns and Beer-Houses that once served Hull`s Old Town. Richard

Hayton. Local History Unit, Hull College, revised edition 1996; Postcard Publishers of Hull & the East Riding 1900 - 1960. Renton Heathcote, privately published by the author, Anlaby, 1994; Chicken Joe: The Man You All Know. C. Ketchell. Local History Archives Unit, Humberside College of Higher Education, Hull, 1986; The Park Street Trail. C. Ketchell. Local History Archives Unit, Hull College of Further Education, 1989; An Illustrated History of the Avenues and Pearson Park: From Victorian Suburb to Conservation Area. (ed.) C. Ketchell. Avenues and Pearson Park Residents Association, Hull, 1989; F.S. Smith`s Drawings of Hull: Images of Victorian Hull 2. C. Ketchell. Hull City Museums & Art Galleries and the Hutton Press, 1990; 'Tremendous Actvity in the Old Town' Demolitions Loss List: List of Buildings demolished in Hull 1941-1990. C. Ketchell. Local History Archives Unit, Hull College of Further Education and Help! Conservation Action Group, Hull, 1990; 'The Blackfriars Archaeological Excavation'. C. Ketchell in Hull Civic Society Newsletter September 1994; "A Spacious Thoroughfare and Handsome Villa Residences": Anlaby Road and Boulevard. notes for local history walk 2 August 1995. C. Ketchell and A. Medforth. Local History Unit, Hull College, 1995; The Dirty Lane and The Fine Thoroughfare: Prince`s Avenue. notes for local history walk 19 June 1996. C. Ketchell. Local History Unit, Hull College, 1996; "In the country yet near the town": A Walk through the Nineteenth Century. The History of Spring Bank. notes for "Walk Right Back" local history walk 7 August 1996. C. Ketchell. Local History Unit, Hull College, 1996; Postcards from Hull & the East Riding. C. Ketchell. Hull Daily Mail Special Supplement, 1996; Postcards from Hull & The East Riding 2. C. Ketchell. Hull Daily Mail Special Supplement, 1996; Humberside in the First World War. S. Kimberley. Local History Archives Unit, Humberside College of Higher Education, Hull, 1988; The Day The Russian Imperial Fleet Fired on the Hull Trawlermen 1904. B. Lewis, D. Prudhoe, J. Billingham, and C. Ketchell. A People`s History of Yorkshire, City of Hull Museums and Art Galleries, Hull 1983; Hull Street Shrines & Rolls of Honour. M. & M. Mann, privately published by the authors, Hull, 1993; Streets of Hull: A History of their Names. John Markham. Highgate Publications (Beverley) Ltd., new edition, 1990; Lost Churches & Chapels of Hull. D. Neave, with G. Bell, C. Ketchell and S. Neave. Hutton Press Ltd., Cherry Burton, 1991; An Historical Atlas of East Yorkshire. (eds.) Susan Neave and Stephen Ellis. The University of Hull Press, 1996; 'The Actual Boot': The Photographic Postcard Boom 1900-1920. Martin Parr and Jack Stasiak. A.H. Jolly (Editorial) Ltd., Northampton in association with The National Museum of Photography Film & Television, Bradford, 1986; Yorkshire: York and the East Riding. Nikolaus Pevsner and David Neave. The Buildings of England series Penguin Books, second edition, 1995; Photographs and Local History. George Oliver. Batsford Local History Series, B.T. Batsford Ltd., 1989; Victorian & Edwardian Photographers in Kingston upon Hull & Beverley. Michael Pritchard. The Royal Photographic Society Historical Group, Bath/Malet Lambert Local History Reprints, Hull, 1984; The Hull Dock Offices 1787-1976. John H. Rumsby. City of Kingston upon Hull Museums & Art Galleries, 1976; IPM Catalogue of Picture Postcards and Year Book, 1989. J.H.D. Smith. IPM Publications, Brighton, 1988; Hull in the 1950s: A Pictorial Diary of Life in Kingston upon Hull. John E. Smith. Hutton Press Ltd., Cherry Burton, 1994; Hull Docklands: An Illustrated History of the Port of Hull. Michael Thompson. Hutton Press Ltd., Cherry Burton, 1990; Andrew Marvell & His Wandering Statue. G. Watkins. Hull City Museums, Art Galleries and Archives, Hull, 1995; Brown`s Illustrated Guide to Hull. E. Wrigglesworth, Hull, 1891 reprinted EP Publishing Ltd., East Ardsley, 1972; More Illustrated History of the Railways of Hull. W.B. Yeadon. Challenger Publications, Oldham, 1995.